FINGERPAINTING

on the

MOON

FINGERPAINTING

on the

MOON

☾

WRITING AND CREATIVITY
AS A PATH TO FREEDOM

PETER LEVITT

HARMONY BOOKS
NEW YORK

The author gratefully acknowledges the following publishers and persons for granting permission to reprint:

Eight lines from "Song" from *Selected Poems 1947–1995* by Allen Ginsberg. Copyright © 1996 by Allen Ginsberg. Reprinted by permission of HarperCollins Publishers Inc. From *Odes to Common Things* by Pablo Neruda. Copyright © 1941 by Pablo Neruda and Fundación Pablo Neruda (Odes Spanish); copyright © 1994 by Ken Krabbenhoft (Odes English Translation); copyright © 1994 by Ferris Cook (Illustrations and Compilation). Reprinted by permission of Little, Brown and Company, Inc. "Inteligencia, Dame" Copyright: Herederos de Juan Ramón Jiménez. Reprinted by permission of Herederos de Juan Ramón Jiménez. *The Book of Questions* by Pablo Neruda © 1991 by William O'Daly with permission generously granted by Copper Canyon Press. Robert Creeley for "The Warning" from *The Collected Poems of Robert Creeley 1945–1975* © 1982, the Regents of the University of California. Lew Welch "(I Saw Myself)" from *Ring of Bone* © 1979, by kind permission of Don Allen and Grey Fox Press. Michael Wenger and San Francisco Zen Center for quote by Shunryu Suzuki-roshi and his translation of lines by Tozan. Daniel Ladinsky for the Hafiz poem from *The Gift*, by Daniel Ladinsky. Copyright © 1999 by Daniel Ladinsky. Reprinted by permission of the author. Four-line excerpt from "Canto CXX" by Ezra Pound, from *The Cantos of Ezra Pound*, copyright © 1934, 1937, 1940, 1948, 1956, 1959, 1962, 1963, 1966, and 1968 by Ezra Pound. Reprinted by permission of New Directions Publishing Corp. "Danse Russe" by William Carlos Williams, from *Collected Poems: 1909–1939, Volume I*, copyright © 1938 by New Directions Publishing Corp. Reprinted by permission of New Directions Publishing Corp. "Often I Am Permitted to Return to a Meadow" by Robert Duncan, from *The Opening of the Field*, copyright © 1960 by Robert Duncan. Reprinted by permission of New Directions Publishing Corp. Howard Norman for "Larger Ears" and "Born Tying Knots" from *The Wishing Bone Cycle*, copyright © 1976 by Howard A. Norman.

Published by Harmony Books, New York, New York. Member of the Crown Publishing Group, a division of Random House, Inc.

www.randomhouse.com

HARMONY BOOKS is a registered trademark and the Harmony Books colophon is a trademark of Random House, Inc.

Printed in the United States of America

Design by Meryl Sussman Levavi

Library of Congress Cataloging-in-Publication Data
Levitt, Peter.
Fingerpainting on the moon : writing and creativity as a path to freedom / Peter Levitt.—1st ed.
p. cm.
1. Authorship. 2. Creative ability. I. Title.
PN145.L385 2003
808'.02—dc21 2002155595
ISBN 0-609-61048-1

10 9 8 7 6 5 4 3 2 1

First Edition

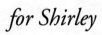

for Shirley

ACKNOWLEDGMENTS

I offer my deepest gratitude and love to my wife, Shirley Graham, for the creative, spiritual, emotional, and practical support she gave me during the writing of this book. I was always able to depend upon her wisdom, her poetic spirit and understanding, and her profound caring for me, our family, and the interests of readers. This would be quite a different book—and quite a different life—without the generosity of Shirley's wise and loving touch, and I thank her with all my heart.

My love and thanks also go to Tai, Sheba, and Mike for their joyous, deep-hearted spirits and generous offerings. To have such children leading the way is a blessing indeed.

I want to thank other dear friends for their love, guidance, and the spiritual and creative companionship that in particular deeply enriched the journey of this book. For the many days and nights of good food and drink, countless great conversations, and not a little shared meditation, I offer my love and blessings to Peter Schnitzler, Deena Metzger, Michael Ortiz Hill, Jonathan Omerman, Nan Gefen, Stephen Nachmanovitch, Leslie Blackhall, Kim Baer, Tom Vinetz, Frank and Annica Burnaby, Matthew and Phyllis Coleman, and Don Singer. I send a special thanks to Ken Kobland for dusting me off.

To Jakusho Kwong-roshi, who has been both teacher and friend, and who has offered so much to help develop my understanding, I offer nine bows. I thank Taizan Maezumi-roshi, Dainin Katagiri-roshi, and Thich Nhat Hanh for their guidance and kind teachings, and Joanna Macy and Kaz Tanahashi for their dear friendship and the courage to live their visions in ways that so inform my life.

To the other poets, artists, writers, and dharma friends with whom I have traveled this road, I offer my thanks and deep appreciation, and most particularly I offer my love and gratitude to Diane Di Prima and Robert Creeley for their early inspiration, generosity, and the company of their friendship all these years.

I am blessed in having Anne Edelstein as my agent and thank her for her always wise advice, support, friendship, and faith in my work. It was Anne who brought the manuscript to Linda Loewenthal at Harmony Books, and I can't thank her enough. Linda's deep belief in this book and the enthusiasm and support she offered went straight to my heart. Her insightful editing and shaping of the material is present on

Acknowledgments

virtually every page. So many thanks. I am also deeply grateful to Shaye Areheart, who came in toward the very end and, under enormous pressure, edited brilliantly while supporting the vision of this book with sensitive, knowing, and appreciative eyes.

Many years ago, Kwong-roshi said, "Please be a good student so I can be a good teacher." I have been blessed with "good students" for thirty years, and, truth to tell, without them my whole approach to teaching—which shaped and informed much of the content of this book—would not have been possible. My hope is that if they find this book in their hands, they will accept it as an acknowledgment of their contribution and as an offering of friendship and thanks.

Precious little of my teaching would have taken place without the gracious and dedicated support given by Ann Colburn and the late Barbara Strauss. For the more than twenty years of opening their homes to poetry on a weekly basis, I offer my gratitude and love.

I also offer my appreciation to Patrick Lannan and the Lannan Foundation for the crucial support given in material and invisible ways.

Finally, to my parents, Jesse and Tillie Levitt: Because you always wanted the best for me, I learned to want it for myself and for everyone. In ways that are both mysterious and known, I became a poet and teacher rooted in a spiritual life as a result of your loving home. May the teachings in this book honor even some small part of what you gave.

CONTENTS

Contents

AUTHOR'S NOTE

AWAKENING JOY

A number of years ago I received a message from a woman who had signed up for my translation workshop; let's call her Jane. For more than thirty years I have been working with writers, artists, and others who want to explore their creative depths, and I intended for this workshop to be a new approach. I could feel the urgency behind Jane's message, so I quickly returned her call.

When she answered the phone she sounded as if I were 911 calling her back. She spoke all in one breath, saying that before signing up she had not read the class description but now she realized we were going to translate contemporary French, Spanish, and Polish poetry and work with poems from eighth-century China and thirteenth-century Japan. As she spoke, Jane's voice wound so tightly into the upper registers that she finally began to laugh.

I listened quietly, compassionately, hearing her terror and sensing that it could be the springboard for enormous joy.

"That's right," I told her. "It's pretty exciting stuff."

"But I don't know any of those languages!" she said, as if one of us were insane. "I don't know anything about ancient China. I couldn't tell you where Vietnam is on a map."

I couldn't resist playing it straight to the end, so I said, "Well, that shouldn't be a problem." I spoke in a genuine but lighthearted way. "We won't be working from Vietnamese."

"No problem?" she cried. "How am I going to do the work if I don't know the languages?"

"It will be okay," I told her. "You don't need any previous experience with these languages, only a willingness to practice fingerpainting on the moon. How does that sound? It's a lot easier than learning Chinese."

It was a remarkable moment. She exploded with a sigh of joy and surprise.

"It sounds great," she said. I had an image of her lifting off the ground. "I have no idea what it is, but I'm sure I can do it!"

"I'm happy to hear it," I said. "And by the way, try not to worry. You already know how."

"I do?" she said. She was starting to worry.

"Sure. You've known it forever. It's part of your joy."

Jane laughed again, this time more relaxed, and said, "Oh, boy. Here we go." And then we hung up.

Just before taking up something new, a whole constellation of thoughts and feelings gathers in our hearts and minds. I am sure you have felt this many times. We feel excited, anxious, frightened, hopeful. It's quite natural for these feelings to run away with us, to become interchangeable and confused. This is part of what happens when the realm of possibility nears. Often, however, another feeling calls to us quietly. It speaks in the way certain ocean stones do with their color and shine. This is joy—the kind that comes from expressing the most intimate part of our lives and having it valued and known. Awakening such joy allows us to love. For many of us, painting, writing, sculpting, dancing, and all the other forms of creative expression are ways to show love to the world. It is to these forms of love and to your willingness to bring them into your life that I dedicate the teachings in *Fingerpainting on the Moon*.

Of all the poems I know, one of the most exuberant and beautiful demonstrations of the simple joy of creating was written by William Carlos Williams. It is called "Danse Russe." I love it because the picture of the artist it presents extends permission to each of us to find some way to speak from the depths of who we are. I love imagining the joy he must have felt when writing this poem. I am also grateful for the wisdom it provides. Here is how it ends:

> *if I in my north room*
> *dance naked, grotesquely*
> *before my mirror*

waving my shirt round my head
and singing softly to myself:
"I am lonely, lonely.
I was born to be lonely,
I am best so!"
If I admire my arms, my face
my shoulders, flanks, buttocks
against the yellow drawn shades,—

Who shall say I am not
the happy genius of my household?

THE PATH OF JOY

I have written this book to help readers become the happy geniuses of their households. It includes many of the treasured stories, anecdotes, teachings, insights, and exercises that have been essential to my life as a poet and a teacher. My students have told me that these have proven crucial to their creative and spiritual lives as well. I intend for the beginning chapters to inspire you to take risks and to help you give yourself permission to do the creative work you want and need to do. Part of this permission depends upon your knowing that while you may not always feel that it is true, you were born to create. It is your birthright, your nature. Remember: *Everything is permitted in the imagination.*

I will also talk about the internal critics we all share. I call them *hungry ghosts.* These are the ones that try to prevent you from expressing the bare root of what you are in your

work and other parts of your life. Once these are fully understood, and you learn the simple methods I offer to free up
those parts of yourself that feel hesitant, unworthy, or afraid,
you will be amazed at the vitality that will permeate everything you create.

Painters Paul Klee, Kazuaki Tanahashi, and Henri Matisse are part of these early chapters. So are Saint Francis, various Zen masters who offer their practical wisdom, and Hillel
the Elder, the renowned Jewish teacher who lived at the time
of Herod. They will show you how to step forward and put
new ground beneath your feet every moment of your life.

Throughout this book you will be offered opportunities
to integrate the teachings with the contents of your imagination and the needs of your deepest self. Most often this will be
done through experiential exercises and writing. I refer to "the
writer" in various paragraphs because writing has been my primary form of creative expression, but this book is not for writers alone. It is not meant to help you develop perfect prose or
poetry, though writers will definitely find their work more
expressive and real. All who long to return to their creative
source and to express both the journey and what they find
once they are there will be able to use this book.

If you prefer painting, sculpting, or dancing to the written word, please read the chapters and then be the happy
genius of your household in any way that expresses who you
are. Even readers who never do the exercises can benefit. If
you just want to read a chapter and then sit quietly or take a
walk, please feel free. My hope was to write a book that
reflects the treasure you already have and to show you new

ways to use it. There are countless ways to practice finger-painting on the moon.

One of the joys of making this book was the company I got to keep. It was also the knowledge that eventually you would meet this company. It was like preparing a banquet. In addition to those I've already mentioned, Pablo Neruda, Allen Ginsberg, Itzhak Perlman, and Sufi poets Rumi and Hafiz will inspire you and show you how to use what they have offered. They will join Eihei Dōgen, Teilhard de Chardin, and other Christian, Jewish, Buddhist, Sufi, Hindu, and Native American teachers, artists, and mystics in an ongoing demonstration of creativity and spirit. Their visions, interpretations, and wisdom will help you to express yourself in ways that are authentic and real. They are true teachers of the path to freedom and joy.

A LUCKY MAN

I have made a life out of writing and teaching. Or perhaps I should say that writing and teaching have made my life what it is. These creative disciplines have required me to be fully present with whatever comes my way. They have asked me to commit to being intimate with every part of myself and to expand my idea of what I am to include all things. In making these demands, they have been spiritual teachers that have taken me to the center of who I am. This kind of intimacy may sound frightening to some, but I can assure you that it is the natural outcome of your willingness to fingerpaint on the moon. Every chapter you read will help you to do this, and I am sure you will welcome the freedom it brings.

I have been a poet for almost forty years. There are people who say they were born poets or artists, but I am not one of these. I had to come to it when I was a young man, already married, and found there was nothing else I really loved or seemed to be able to do. It may sound like a wonderful realization—and in its own way it was—but it was also an agonizing moment of self-revelation when I finally knew that, against all odds, what I loved doing most in the world was making a poem. A *poet*, for God's sake! I could hardly say the word. But by then I knew that even making a bad poem—which I was very good at—was better than not making one at all. *Love is love,* I used to tell myself. There is often little we can do.

During this time I fed what I called *my poetry habit* by reading as much poetry, literature, and spiritual teaching as I could. I found that these diverse readings awakened my intuition and nourished each other in unpredictable ways. I also began my practice of meditation. Working in this way was a bit like weaving a tapestry where the next thread just appears in your hand, which is what happens when your intuition and imagination become fully alive. You don't necessarily know how the new thread is going to fit into the design, but because your mind welcomes whatever appears, more often than not it does. This inclination has proven so trustworthy that I continue to rely upon it in my teaching and writing to this day. It is how I gathered the material and wrote the chapters you are about to read. It was part of the joy. As you read the various stories and teachings, and work with the creative suggestions I have made, you may find exactly what you need appearing in your hands. You may also be surprised to discover that you know exactly how it fits.

From time to time threads appear that shine with a special brilliance and imbue the entire fabric with their light. They seem to show up at will and are so definitive that they help us to make sense of the whole design. These often take the form of a phrase we read or overhear, or they show up as a spontaneously created image in our painting or poem. Whatever their source, we experience them so deeply that we stop right where we are.

This is how our imagination catches our attention. When we stop and give ourselves permission to risk seeing what is really here before us, we are answering one of life's deepest calls. It is a call that rises from our yearning to be whole. I have tried to write this book in a way that places many such threads before you. Some may shine more brightly for you than others, but when taken together, they will lead you to truths about yourself you may need to know. They may even take you to the creative source of your life right where you stand.

Let me give you an example. In my own early years a thread of this order came to me as a few lines by William Carlos Williams. His poetry was fairly new to me in those days, but I loved how he made the world of his poems so real.

> *I am a poet! I*
> *am. I am. I am a poet, I reaffirmed, ashamed*

When I read these words at the age of twenty-one, I heard in my heart the insistent rhythm of *"I am. I am. I am . . ."* Williams had so perfectly mirrored what I felt myself to be that I knew I would never veer from this life I loved. I had joined, or hoped to join, a club of the hopeless, and my spirit soared with joy.

AS JOY APPROACHES

All authentic creative acts rise from our deepest self, the place where imagination and spirit are born. Imagination and spirit are twin reflections of our relationship to the self, and though not identical, they cannot be separated. We even speak of the *spirit of imagination* that a work of art contains. If we live in a way that crushes our spirit, our imagination may be damaged to the same degree. No matter what creative form we choose, our truest work comes about when we nourish who we are. This is the root of true and intimate expression.

But we don't write, paint, sculpt, or create music and dance solely to express what resides at the core of our lives. Creative acts can reveal the content of who and what we are by bringing us face-to-face with our true nature. Our yearning for wholeness uses our intuition, our dreams, and our creative work to bring us home. When discovery and expression appear in one bold stroke, our hidden self leaps into our hands.

Many people think that the kind of exploration I've been discussing rules out joy. They believe that nothing of a serious nature will come about if we do not *get down to business and steel ourselves to the task.* Nothing could be further from the truth. Things tend to work better when we use a lighter touch. It's a bit like handling a large ball of yarn we want to unravel. If we hold the yarn in one hand and pull the end of the loose strand hard, what started out as a simple problem may be instantly transformed into a disaster. The yarn will form a solid knot at the core, and it will be very difficult to sort it out. But if we hold the ball of yarn lightly and give it a little shake, the entanglements tend to sort themselves out, and pretty soon the way to the center becomes clear. Then we can follow the strands to where they lead us and set the whole ball free. When we approach our work and our lives in such a way, joy appears.

AND NOW JOY

I have woven stories from my own life and from the lives of my students, family, and friends into the teachings you are about to read. Some provide an intimate view. Intimacy is at the heart of all creative and spiritual journeys—it is the goal for many, but it is the way for all. Our willingness to live intimately with all things helps to open the secret treasure of our lives. As you turn now to the opening chapter, I offer this anecdote as one of the keys.

I was speaking with a rabbi friend some time ago about what mystical Judaism calls the hidden names of God. In this tradition it is said that the name of the Divine cannot truly be known. *Oneness, the Divine Plenty, the Infinite, the Nameless One*—these and many other names have been offered for what cannot be named. I told my friend that I loved that we try to say what can't be said and hear what can't be heard. It's a good sign—a sign that in our species creativity is well and alive.

"But," I said, "I am sometimes daunted by such grand names. I prefer a simpler name, one that rolls off the tongue. One I can say on a train."

When my friend heard this he looked at me with great excitement. The love he feels for the world filled his eyes.

"But didn't you know?" he said. "It's the secret of secrets, the joy of joys: One of the hidden names is *Yes!* And another is *Now!*"

FINGERPAINTING

on the

MOON

STARTING
IN SILENCE

☽

When I was very young I would ask my mother to tell me stories about her own childhood. More often than not, I would already be in bed with the lights turned out and the warmth of my mother beside me filling the room. I loved to imagine her life, to hear her say the simple phrases that brought before my eyes the mythic landscape of what came before me. I loved to hear about the *trolley car,* the *ice man,* the *milk buckets.* It made me laugh against all reason to imagine my mother as a young girl *shoveling coal,* but it frightened me to picture her standing alone in a dark tenement hallway where she *washed dishes at the sink that five families shared.* Each of the phrases she used called deeply to my imagination and took on the power of a constellation in the sky of my childhood dreams. *Milk bucket* stood beside *ice man. Trolley car* was coming to take him home. And I was there, too, with my mother at my side, taking in the nighttime mystery of where I came from and what the world was like before I was born.

One part of this ritual that I most remember was my mother's silence. Before she spoke, she would always sit quietly for a few moments on the edge of my bed. I could hear in the dark the slightest trace of her breathing. There was something special about this, something almost prayerful in the way she returned to her own beginnings and allowed the images she would speak to fill her eyes and imagination. I could feel her do this, and it made the silence in the room feel almost holy. It was a silence filled with a curious kind of yearning. A silence made of memory, of wonder, and because she always told me true stories, it was also a silence made of pain. *Life is big,* it told me. *Very big. This is something you will come to understand.* And then she would begin to speak.

People have always sought the story of their beginning. It is a primordial yearning at the root of all creation myths. As individuals and cultures we have been fascinated with the nature of how we and the world came to be. It is a primary source of our expressive arts. Once our intuition finds its way into form, we begin the naming by which we place ourselves among all other things in the world, what native people of the First Nation call *all my relations.* Our creations provide a sense of order and meaning that assures us and those who see our work that we do not face our lives alone. What I was able to feel in my mother's silence is true. *Life is big.* It is bigger than we fully understand. This is part of why we seek to hear and tell stories that take us to our source. We yearn for the intimacy of being wrapped in the sacred shawl such stories provide. And no matter what part of the world, or what tradition, the story comes from, we can tell when it is true.

One story of the beginning of the universe that I have always loved comes from mystical Judaic sources. It says that as you stand beneath a midnight sky and gaze into the heavens, each of the countless stars above you and the entire dark fabric of night in this never-ending shimmer dance of black and white before your eyes carries within it a spark of the original Creator. It tells us that at the beginning of creation itself, a lit ember of the Divine was sewn like a stitch into every element that makes up this quilt of night and stars.

As you stand in the presence of this illuminated sky that is at once familiar and mysterious, it is very easy to believe this is so. But the story does not stop there. The tradition holds that this ember, this creative spark of the Divine, is not reserved solely for the marvels seen in the heavens at night— the spinning planets, the shooting stars; all things of the universe, including ourselves, are vessels that carry the creative spark. The hidden stitch of light sewn into the fabric of all life is part of who and what we are.

This teaching of the universality of creative sparks implies that whether we are answering the telephone, changing the baby, riding the subway, or writing a poem, we are in touch with the creative source of life itself. Everything we encounter provides the same opportunity for us to meet the creative source: the play of early morning sunlight on our eyelids, the smooth cloth of the pillowcase beneath our cheek, the cutting of carrots and celery. But we must remember that being in touch with the creative is not just a matter of what we come upon as we move through our day. It is right here, the teaching says, in ourselves. When we learn to see with the eyes of the creative itself, every moment is an opportunity for new expression. We are always standing at a gateway of awe.

Mystical Jewish teachings can be quite compelling. At least part of their intent is to light a pathway that people may follow to the source of creation and life itself. At times the teachings can be quite provocative. Most of us who are familiar with the Old Testament are aware that when the Divine first speaks out of the Great Silence of the void, the words *"Let there be light!"* resound through all parts of the beginning world. We also know that the phrase that follows this command is *"And there was light!"* In the tradition, this light was brought into existence by the divinely spoken words. This is the root of the mystical belief that since God articulated the entirety of the creation into existence, every element of the visible and invisible worlds—all physical matter in the universe—is comprised of the original letters of the Hebrew alphabet spoken *in the beginning* by the Great Creator. In other words, we and everything we encounter—every tree, every flower, every birdsong; every grain of wheat that ends up on our breakfast table; every glance and gesture we see and make during the day, and even the atoms of air within which we move our bodies—are originally made of a divinely articulated alphabet created by the Source of Life.

I first encountered this teaching in a conversation with a friend. Initially, I could hardly make sense of it at all. We even laughed together as I tried to imagine what letters made up my mouth and nose. My friend was a gentle guide, however, and in between bouts of laughter he told me a few of the letters that constituted the area around my eyes and what the tradition says they mean. I listened carefully, because the interpretations were beginning to appeal to me. They possessed a certain quality that awakened my intuition and faced me in the creative and spiritual direction I call *home.*

After my friend left, I went outside to stand on the bridge that separated my house from the road and looked up at the sky. It was one of those clear nights of early winter, very cold. The Milky Way flowed above me like a river of stars. I let myself begin to absorb what I had been told by imagining that the heavens were an immense ark that held the sacred scrolls of the Torah, the Jewish Law. Fairly soon I saw that the ark held an illuminated scroll of white letters written on the black papyrus of space, and that this papyrus was also made of letters, ones I couldn't see as it turned endlessly throughout all time. *It's an alphabet of stars,* I told myself. I was amazed. Since it really was quite cold I started back to the house, and as I did I looked at a more familiar world. The towering sycamore and pine. The river that ran beside my home. My hand. *It could be,* I thought. *How wonderful. We are surrounded by the mystery of unrecognized words.*

It is a remarkable thing to realize for any artist. For anyone. To grasp even a little of what this implies can make quite a difference in how we move through the world, seeing what we see and hearing what we hear. It opens our hearts and excites possibility in our imagination. Suddenly, the source of life appears within reach. *"You hold the book of creation in your hand,"* my friend told me. *"Look at it. Learn to read the book."*

Our rational minds may not know how to respond, but years of writing and teaching has made it clear to me that some part of us does know. It is our deepest self. It uses such teachings to awaken the unified voice of our intuition and our yearning for wholeness. When this voice becomes sufficiently aroused, it begins to speak. *I have something for you,* it says. *Something you will love. Something you can use for your next creation. Something that will take you home. Come closer.*

Sometimes we can hear this voice. After all, it is our true self speaking and is rooted in something very large. More often than not, we are unaware that we are even being called. In part this is because we keep a distance between ourselves and our world. We feel our safety depends upon it. We close our eyes to the creative spark all things contain and tell ourselves we don't have the interest or the time. But we are only turning a blind eye to ourselves. It is a risky thing to do. And it is the wrong risk to take.

It is in the spirit of awe, inspiration, yearning, and the need we all have to discover the light of the creative sparks in our lives that I urge you to close the gap and give yourself entirely to all parts of your world. When you do, your work will be intimate and true. It will take a risk, to be sure—but it is a risk whose name is discovery and joy. Then you will begin to unravel the mystery of unrecognized words and learn to read the book of creation.

But who has written this book?
It is you.
And who will read it?
The you in everyone who holds it in their hands.
And how can it be understood?
Ah! The mystery becoming known.
But is it real? Is it me?
Only give yourself to the book and you will know.
But what will I know? How will I know it?
Welcome home!

RISK

(

A lone syllable. A single word. Sometimes a noun. Always, in the heart of it, a verb. All creative expression depends upon our willingness to take a risk, and yet just to say the word creates a feeling of excitement and fear in most people, a sense of danger rooted in the threat of change. Years ago I was told a story in which the painter Paul Klee said, *"When I paint what you know, I bore you. And when I paint what I know, I bore me. So I paint what I don't know."* Isn't that wonderful? Paint or write what you don't know. *Create what you have not even begun to suspect!* This is risk. It is the freeing intent behind most original work. According to Klee, the means to help our deepest selves make their mark in the world is right here in the tip of our innocent pencil or brush—the one we hold in our hand—if only we will risk.

Often, however, we avoid taking this first step, and therefore never get to the last. We convince ourselves that conditions are not exactly right or that some special moment of inspiration or insight must occur before we can create. In order to help you move past such hesitation—which can last a lifetime if you allow it to grab hold of your life—let me tell you what writer, painter, and calligrapher Kazuaki Tanahashi had to say in his book *Brush Mind*: "*There is no need to imagine before you paint. Painting brings forth imagination.*" In other words, no special conditions are needed. This was his way of encouraging us to have confidence in the life-giving capacity of risk. It has been proven time and time again. One brush stroke leads to another. One written word calls forth the next. All we have to do is begin.

Our willingness to risk brings the moment, ourselves, and our work to life in a way that did not exist just seconds before. It can be very exhilarating and powerful when risk taking ignites us into the new. But, of course, while risk does create life, death is also present as a possibility. Often, just before we risk something in our lives, even something small, the fear of dying can be found.

It is only natural to feel this way, especially since in creative work something does die. Something must die for our work to create something new, even if it is only an old idea. The key is to risk everything, to let everything go and die into our work, as Tanahashi does when he paints. It was to honor this quality in him that I wrote this poem:

The painter dies
with each brushstroke.
That's how he came
to be so old.

By now we have all lived long enough to discover that one gateway to freedom depends upon our ability to alter how we look at what is right before us. When we do, what has previously blocked our way appears to unlock itself, as if by sleight of hand. As it says in the Heart Sutra chanted in Zen temples around the world, when there is no hindrance in the mind, there is no hindrance at all, and therefore no fear exists. What a joy it is when the wall falls down or the seemingly impenetrable dissolves. This is a kind of dying; it is the dying of one or more beliefs that were never more than illusions that whispered in our ear with such authority we took them for real.

Light as they might appear, however, these illusions wield a heavy power over our psyches, and it takes the strong medicine of risk to unseat them. When we make risk our ally an onrush of creative, life-affirming energy becomes available to us equal to the amount that had been held in check. Then the environment of our inner lives becomes more free and feels instantly permeated with a sense of rightful peace. Such freedom is what it is all about.

What I love about Klee's commitment is the freedom it provided him as an artist to fully explore what he, in that very moment, proved to be. Freedom frees everything it moves through, everything it touches. Look at the playful quality of the paintings for which Klee is mostly known and you will discover in his use of color and form precisely what I mean. The freedom he experienced while painting permeates the work itself and becomes part of the viewer's experience as well. For us to know such freedom, our creative work must be a vital, visceral act of exploration. It cannot just be a rehashing of what has already occurred, or what we have previously thought or said. Don't forget, the word *predictable* means "said before." William Carlos Williams pointed to this essential characteristic of composition when he said that the poet thinks with the poem, *"and that,* in itself, *is the profundity."* (The emphasis here is mine.) This sensibility reveals a primary reason we love to write or paint or engage in any form of expressive creation: *The meaning is earned in the act of composition itself.* This changes how our work is usually seen. It is no longer simply the vehicle of expression, but the skillful means by which we discover and explore the deepest truths of what we are. Risk, which is needed for us to become intimate with what is solid and real within us, is at the fore.

TWO ZEN STORIES

One day a nun was walking in the mountains near a cliff when suddenly she felt the ground slip from beneath her feet. She experienced herself falling, and at the last moment, as she fell, she grabbed on to a branch that was sticking out from the side of the cliff. Frightened, she called out, "Help! Help!" but no one else was around to hear her. After some time a teacher and some students who were walking nearby heard her cries and came to the edge of the cliff. When the nun saw them she shouted, "Please!

You've got to help me!" The teacher looked at the situation and said to her, "Just let go!" (Isn't that wonderful? "Just let go!") The nun was terrified because she knew she was hanging vertically in midair, high above the ground, and yet this teacher was telling her to let go. "I can't!" she cried. But the teacher was very kind, and very firm, and told her, "You've got to let go! Without any hesitation, you've got to let go now!" So she did. The nun let go and found that she had not been hanging vertically in midair after all. The entire time she had been lying horizontally on the ground, and the ground had been supporting her all along.

This second story is also based on a traditional teaching from the Zen tradition. It has been such an essential part of my own understanding of creativity and life for so many years I can't recall where I first heard it.

One day, toward the end of the year when his modest temple was about to close during the most difficult weeks of winter, a disciple of an old and venerated Zen master invited his teacher to stay with him at his family's humble home situated in the nearby mountains. The Zen master agreed and the two of them set out. As the disciple led his master along a mountain path during their journey to his home, they found themselves gradually enveloped in a fog that whitened the mountain air and made it impossible to see more than two steps ahead. Nevertheless, without the slightest resistance on the part of the old man, the disciple led his teacher forward into the thickening fog. Suddenly, with his teacher at his side, the disciple felt his foot slip and grabbed his teacher's kimono to keep from falling into what turned out to be a deep abyss of ice and snow that lay at their feet. When they looked at what was right before them, the disciple realized he had lost his way and, in his confusion, had brought his teacher to the edge of a treacherous cliff. "I'm sorry," he said, feeling somewhat frightened and ashamed. "I seem to have lost my way in the mountain and have no idea where we are." The teacher looked at his young student for only a moment, and then turned his old eyes back to the snowed-in valley below. "Jump!" he said. "Take my hand and jump from this ledge if you value your life and mine." The disciple could barely believe his ears, but, despite his terrible fear and the shaking of his bones, he did exactly as his teacher said. Grabbing the hand of the person he most trusted in the world, he jumped from the icy cliff and in the very next second discovered that he and his teacher were walking, hand in hand, on the sun-drenched road that led to the village where he was born.

As these stories show, risk implies that something we hold dear may be threatened. Perhaps it is our lives. But, as I've said, this is precisely where a writer wants to be. The truth is that the riskiest thing a writer can do is to try to be safe. This is the same as deciding to stay within the boundaries of the world the writer already knows. After all, it makes a certain sense, right? Haven't we become experts in that world? Let me answer by saying simply that it is true such boundaries may keep us safe, and that decent work may be found within them, but they also prevent us from discovering the infinite landscape and possibility that our spiritual need and imagination hold for us. And, as for being "experts" of such a proscribed realm, I ask only that you consider this statement from Zen master Shunryu Suzuki-roshi, who said: *"In the beginner's mind there are many possibilities, but in the expert's there are few."*

It is true. Just as every heartbeat and breath is the agency of a new beginning in our lives, taking a risk is the very same agency for maintaining a beginner's mind with every word we write.

I think it is fair at this point to ask what part of ourselves wants us to wander endlessly in the land of the known, where, in time, even we will begin to believe the world is flat. What wants to keep us from discovering the content of our being that most yearns to be discovered? Whom does it serve— always a good question to ask—when we are held at such a distance from ourselves?

Time and again, over the years, writers I have worked with have shown me perfectly authentic, driving, inventive work that suddenly—sometimes even in the middle of a phrase—dies right before my eyes. Whether what they were writing was based on some particularly painful or confusing aspect of their lives, or was rooted in parts of themselves that had never previously been expressed, or even the urgent need for answers from some spiritual quest, it is the same. No matter how powerful the initial impulse to finally get it said, the life dwindles out of the writing and it dies.

I remember one poem in which a writer who had lost quite a few members of her family in the concentration camps of eastern Europe was finally expressing her anger at God, fifty years in the making. Suddenly, in the middle of this cry torn from the burning ground of her life, just as the poem was about to finally give voice to parents, uncles, aunts, and cousins whose own voices had been turned to ash, everything became nice. Very nice. The writer became interested in a vase of daisies on her kitchen table. How beautiful they were. How they caught the sun.

"Just a moment, please," I told her. "I'm reading your poem. Death and rage are in the room. A woman is screaming into the womb of silence left behind by an absent God. Ghosts of family and blood fly through the air like some nightmarish painting by Chagall, and suddenly we're concentrating on these daisies? Which may be lovely, indeed," I assured her. "But *why now?*"

How does this happen? What makes us cut the creative flow of feeling, thought, and association until we subvert the writing with a distraction, or turn off the power that drives the story or poem? Why do we lose access to the vital root of what clearly means so much to us? For most people the answer is quite simple: Intimacy with what is most essential to us dies the instant we feel that our exploration and expression are going into areas that either feel too unfamiliar or that may contain material we fear we cannot control. We would rather derail the forward motion of discovery and avoid taking the risk such intimacy demands than go all the way through to truth. And through truth, to expression. And through expression, to freedom.

But clearly each part of us does not want such subversion. If that were true we wouldn't write a word. Some part of us wants to maintain intimate contact so we may give voice to those parts of ourselves that we are finally coming to know. So what part of us does not want to risk losing control? Who can't bear the threat?

Be very gentle as you ask yourself this question. There is never a need to cause yourself unnecessary fear. Besides, the part of the human psyche that likes things just the way they are, without any uncomfortable revelations, is frightened enough. In a rather lighthearted way I like to think of this particular part of our ego as a bureaucrat who believes its job is to keep its job. Anything that threatens the status quo has got to go. It is allergic to the kind of risk writers must take in the name of authentic writing, the risk that yields the greatest benefit. The last thing it wants is for us to discover the relationship between risk and surrender—as in surrendering to what we don't know—and it will do everything it can to exhaust the psychic and imaginative energy our writing needs so that it may bring this process to a halt.

I characterize our ego in this way to have a little fun, but, as you know, this bureaucrat holds a lot of power. More often than we would wish, our lives are in its control. What we need to do is to step off the ledge of this fearful inclination. Just step right off. This involves both risk and surrender. When we do, we strengthen our intimate connection to what makes authentic expression possible, and, just like the disciple who jumped into the snowy abyss while holding on to the hand of his old master, the one whose beginner's mind was ready for every possibility, we find ourselves walking down the road of unbounded joy that leads to the place where we are born.

HILLEL: THE FIRST ONE-FOOTED JEWISH HAIKU POET

Rabbi Hillel—or Hillel the Elder, as he came to be known in his later years—was the child of a wealthy Babylonian family, born one or two generations before the Common Era. As he matured he gave himself entirely to the study of the Torah, and, after coming to Jerusalem to continue cultivating his soul's depth and understanding, he supported himself as a woodcutter. I can't say for certain that he was a very good woodcutter, for he lived in such great poverty that as a young student he could not even afford the admission fee for study. The seriousness of his intent, however, was so palpable that beginning with Hillel the long-standing tradition of charging this fee was abolished for all who wanted to become intimate with the teachings.

In time, Hillel's reputation as a man of wisdom and gentleness rose to such great heights that he stood at the head of the community as the great spiritual and ethical leader of his generation. This was at about the time when Herod's reign was ending, approximately 10 B.C.E. to 10 C.E. You may have heard of Hillel because he is the person who said, *"If I am not for myself, then who will be for me? And if I am only for myself, then what am I? And if not now, when?"* As you can see, Hillel was a man who placed himself beyond the horizon of safety, well in the land of risk.

I bring Hillel the Elder into this chapter because of a story I find of tremendous inspiration and use. It is told that one day a man came to Hillel and said that he would allow Hillel to convert him if Hillel could teach him the entirety of the Torah while standing on one foot. Hillel is said to have raised one foot off the ground without the slightest hesitation and replied: *"What is hateful to you, do not unto your neighbor; this is the entirety of the Torah. All the rest is commentary. Go study!"*

Given the spontaneity of the rabbi's approach and the depth of his expression, I think there is little question that Hillel and Paul Klee would have gotten along. Painting what you don't know, jumping from icy ledges, releasing your grip from a branch, and standing on one foot while articulating the heart of the Law of your people with spontaneity and confidence are all rooted in the same disposition of mind. But, for now, I want to focus on that singular, physical (some might say metaphysical) foot of this sage. Besides, it will give you an opportunity to move around.

Since we can learn quite a bit about risk from our physical makeup, I ask you to please stand and keep reading. Make sure you have at least four or five feet of clear space in front of you. I'm going to ask you to read this next section through, hold it in your mind as you do what is described, and then pick up the book again. Following these instructions alone already qualifies you as a risk taker. So, here we go.

Stand with your feet at a comfortable distance apart. You may sway a little until your body feels more relaxed and loose. As you stand there I want to remind you that in our culture we have been told time and time again that we have to stand up on our own two feet. *"Chest out, tummy in, get up on your own two feet."* This makes it pretty hard to breathe, or walk, or do just about anything but stand there. Even so, this image is part of the myth of the rugged individualist.

It turns out that even when we appear to be doing something alone it may not really be the case. For example, what are you standing on? Of course you will say you are standing on your feet, and you will be correct in saying so. But what are your feet standing on? If you said the floor or something of that order you would, of course, be correct again. And what is beneath the floor? Yes, it's the earth—or Earth, if you are thinking in a planetary way. And Earth? What is supporting Earth? I think it would be okay to say that Earth is supported by space. And how about space, then? What is space using? Okay, the universe. And how about that? What is holding the universe together?

Do you see how big it can get? Let's call a halt to our investigation here and just say the universe is held together by the laws that govern it, even though we may not understand what they are. So it turns out that while we may appear to be "standing on our own two feet," it takes the floor, the earth, Earth, space, the universe, and the laws that govern all of it for you to be standing right where you are. If any of these are removed I think there is little doubt that you would not be standing there. How's that for feeling supported, for not having to stand alone, or live alone, or write alone? We do not do anything in our lives without the truth of interdependence as an unseen foundation or ground. I like to call this *the ground beneath the ground* because it is always right here doing its job, no matter what we think or say. Nothing exists without it functioning exactly as it does.

If you look deeply at your life and allow this idea of the ground beneath the ground to extend literally and metaphorically, you will find it is the kind of ground upon which Hillel stood. It is no different from the ground of understanding the two Zen masters helped their students to realize. Properly understood, it provides a context for us to see risk in a whole new light.

Time to move. Please slowly shift the weight of your body to one foot. Once that's done, lift the other foot slowly (*very* slowly) and take a slow-motion step forward, bringing your foot to rest on the floor in front of you. Now shift the weight to the foot you've just moved forward, and lift the other foot forward, very slowly, as you take another step. We are really only acting out the process of walking and taking two steps, but in slow motion. With each step, please put your mind in your foot, so to speak, and pay great attention to what you are experiencing in the foot to which you've shifted your weight, the one you've got planted for stability on the ground. Please do this one more time. Take two very slow steps forward (as part of your investigation, you may take three or four steps in this manner if you like), and then come back and read.

Did you notice a slight instability in the foot you were using for balance? Did you notice how as you lifted the other foot to begin your step it may have wobbled a bit, seeking the strength and balance required? Did you also notice how it knew, without being directed by conscious thought, to find its balance and hold its stable position so that the other foot could move forward? If you like, you may do the exercise one more time now to test your experience against what I've said.

Just taking a step can teach us quite a bit about creative process and risk. We move from stability, *through* instability, to stability again. We do it every day thousands of times. Every time we walk we move from a stable position, through one that is less stable, to one that is secure and stable again. It's how we move physically forward in our lives. We're made to do it. We're designed this way.

Our heart beats and stops, beats and stops. It is what pumps blood through our body and keeps us alive. Our lungs breathe in air; then there is a moment between breaths some meditation teachers call *the still point*, a moment during which we are neither breathing in nor out; and then we release the air, having received the nutritious oxygen we need to live. Our eyes open, close, open, close, more times every day than we can count. These are just a few of our natural processes. They do not need to be consciously controlled by intellectual knowing or thought of any kind. They are just the natural functioning of our body, part of the elegant, powerful ground beneath the ground that makes our existence possible.

Thanks to this miraculous design of human beings, systems that do not require the assistance of our beautiful, rational minds help to keep us alive. The same holds true for writing. We do not need to stay in control of every aspect of ourselves in order to write. Quite the opposite. We and our writing really live when "the bureaucrat" takes a break—a long break—during which time we demonstrate to our imagination that we are willing to meet it wherever it says to go. When we do this, our psyche likes it, feels we are trustworthy, and allows us to experience intimately what we really want and need in the exploration and expression of our lives.

Let me use this moment as a reminder: We are not only born to create, we are also born to risk. These are actually the same. Taking a creative risk is not only essential and freeing, it is also the least risky thing you can do. Any attempt to stay safe will never get you where you want to go. But once you become used to risking everything so that authenticity bursts alive in your writing, that pesky bureaucratic part of your ego starts to take credit for it. It really does. It's sort of cute in its transparency, because it sees where you are going and it doesn't want to be left behind. That's why it chases after you shouting, *"See what I did? See where I was willing to go? I risked everything. I did everything. For you!"*

When we write, we are standing on one foot. At first we may be a bit unsure of our ground, but we can have confidence that we are rooted in a ground deeper than we can imagine. If Hillel had allowed the slightest wobble to cause his other foot to come down, we would not have the benefit of his wonderful teaching, or the example of creative and spiritual courage and trust that his act provides. Likewise, if while writing we allow any wobble to throw us off track, we may not discover our own wisdom, our own creative and spiritual courage. Often the burst of energy we feel while taking a risk is the very energy that drives the writing and makes it possible for us to discover and express what has always crouched within, hoping to be found. This is true whether the nature of the energy is fear, anxiety, or excitement of any kind. As Shunryu Suzuki-roshi once said, *"A big block of ice makes a lot of water."*

So we must lift that foot and experience a seeming groundlessness before returning to our ground. When we do return, however, we discover that we are standing on new ground with a strengthened confidence in our spiritual and creative lives. It is a ground of great permission. Frequently, when people first experience the unbounded permission this ground provides, there is laughter, and then there are tears. It is as if all the obstructions in our lives simultaneously disappear. As one student said to me when she discovered this for herself by writing on a painful subject she had avoided for years, *"I just didn't know I could! And even if it was only for a few moments—still, I was free!"* This is pure joy, the kind I imagine Henry Miller must have intended when he subtitled his book of watercolors *Paint* [or in our case, *Write*] *As You Like and Die Happy.*

EVERYTHING IS
PERMITTED IN THE
IMAGINATION

☾

Often I am permitted to return to a meadow
as if it were a scene made-up by the mind,
that is not mine, but is a made place

that is mine, it is so near to the heart
—Robert Duncan

In the meadow outside the room in which I write, the tulips of this extraordinary spring are large enough to hold full portions of wine in their blazing red and yellow bowls. And the daffodils, with their delicate petals of pale white and gold, speak to me of the fragility all life possesses. They seem brave, somehow, determined to live each moment they are given to the fullest. I don't know who originally planted the bulbs that give rise to these flowers year after year, but it feels as if they were geniuses of my own heart and imagination.

One day, during a break in the schedule at the Sonoma Mountain Zen Center, where I have practiced for many years, I was standing in the garden alone. After a brief time, a friend who noticed me standing there came up and said without the slightest introduction, "You know, there's room for us." As she said this she gently swept her hand in an arc to include all the various forms of life before us. I watched as she encircled all the vegetables, fruit and flowers, the compost piles, the shape of the distant mountain, and then included the two of us with her gesturing hand. "If there wasn't room," she said with a conspiratorial smile, "we couldn't be here at all." And then she really smiled.

I didn't reply verbally, but we bowed to each other in unison after she spoke. As I watched her walk away, I felt the true gift she had given with a depth that took me by surprise. *Yes,* I thought. *There is room. Room for every part of life. Even room enough for me.*

There is room in our lives for every image, dream, fantasy, thought, and all the various forms of sensation and imagining that occur. These products of our hearts and imaginations come to us as naturally as the red or golden color that defines the beautiful flowers in the meadow, and, therefore, each one possesses an inherent permission to exist. This is what I mean by "room." No matter how many obstructions are thrown up in an attempt by some fearful part of ourselves to disrupt the natural flow of our expressive lives, no fear, no writer's block, no personal history, no internal conflict or neurosis changes this fact of permission. Of course, in order to truly express our lives we do have to work with such obstructions, and I will continue to offer various creative means for doing so throughout this book, but I say without the slightest hesitation—and because it needs repeating—that the full reach of permission innate to our human existence, like the permission innate to all living things, is absolute. It is an essential attribute of who and what we are.

If you trace the spontaneous content and products of your imagination to their root, you will see that they come from a place so deeply embedded that you cannot even really take credit for them. They just rise in a seeming instant from the ground of our being and take us by surprise. They shock or delight us. They are like gifts from a friend who is either terribly loving or terribly weird, but one who seems in the end to know us well. This is why we cannot credit ourselves with the offerings our psyche provides, and, likewise, we cannot really accept blame for them, either. They just are. If you like, consider one thought red. One image yellow. One dream may be green. Another is blue. We don't really know why. We just think what we think and dream what we dream. Our imaginations freely give us what they want us to have at any given moment for reasons of their own. This is the source of permission that cannot be denied. Our task, then, is to recognize and accept this permission—and the freedom it implies—as part of our life force, and to find a way to use these gifts to further express our lives.

It is precisely because artists have always cultivated their ability to access and express this realm of human freedom that they have been viewed at various times as potentially dangerous to the state, the imposed order from above. For our purposes we might consider the habits and comfort of our own ego structure as "the state." Let's call it *the state of things as they are*. It is *this* state that employs the bureaucrat I mentioned when discussing risk.

Who among us has not felt a certain tremor when this state felt shaken in even the slightest degree? But as writers we do not have a stake in perpetuating the needs of this state. Our way is to be free from all a priori constraints that may have been imposed upon us by others or ourselves and to dive skyward, with a mind clear like space itself, into the unrestricted possibilities of our own imaginings. The more we cultivate our ability to embrace such freedom, the greater our ability to know what we know, and have always known, though we may have had difficulty at times dodging the thought patrol in our attempt to access this knowledge through the heavy veils of constraint.

> *Everything is permitted*
> *Everything is permitted*
> *Everything is permitted in the imagination*

I say it again and again and again.

There is a story related to the T'ang dynasty Chinese poet Wang Wei that I dearly love. In a collection of Wang's poems called *Hiding the Universe,* the editor asks, "*Where do you hide the universe?"* It's a pretty provocative question, I think, and before reading on you might offer a few answers. Where would you hide it? The answer given is one that has always delighted me with its simple clarity: You hide the universe in the universe because that's the only place large enough for it to fit.

I find this as wonderful as it is important for us to know. Since your imagination is as vast as the universe that can only fit within itself, and since it is inherently generous in all normally functioning psyches, it gives you exactly what you need. Of course, sometimes what your imagination thinks you need may appear rather extreme. It has its own way of catching your attention, and some of its methods can be quite provocative. Just think about your most recent frightening or sexual dream and the confusion of feelings it called forth. But these are just some of the methods the imagination has of reeling us in so we will come closer to ourselves and discover the true meaning it wants us to have.

What the imagination really wants is not as complicated or mysterious as you might think. It wants us to readily receive its gifts and the permission inherent in these gifts without judgment. It wants its gifts greeted with an open disposition of heart and mind that allows us to really see what we have been given. When we do so, we encourage the imagination to continue providing us with the very treasures we truly want and need. And it will, because it knows we are listening.

The quality of our listening is crucial to expression. When we listen deeply, giving no concern to previous notions of good and bad, right and wrong, desirable and not, we create a pathway that takes us through the unmapped territory of our deepest selves. This pathway is actually a lifeline to the Creative Source. Once we accept the imagination's gifts *as given,* which depends in part upon our willingness to risk, our writing begins to change. It becomes authentic, charged, and compelling. It possesses a definitive power that drives every image, noun, and verb. As we work with our writing over time, exploring its contents and refining what we discover until what we have written *rings true,* it reveals that we have been expanded to a shape and size more truly our own.

Zen Buddhists say that we are all Buddha, but still we must practice so we can truly realize (make real) the Buddha we are. The same is true for our imagination. It is always here, complete within itself, but we must practice granting ourselves permission to hear it until our imagination gains full expression in our lives. What does it promote, *whom does it serve,* when we block entry, deny permission, and turn our back on this precious gift?

To help you remember this, I would like to make a simple suggestion. Students who have followed this recommendation have been amazed at the relief it provides, especially when life has tied them into knots. (You may read that as *NOTS,* if you prefer.) Make a sign and write in letters big enough for you to see:

PERMISSION GRANTED

As you make this sign, allow everything you've read thus far to crystallize into these two words. Let them signify your commitment to thinking and feeling with a freedom granted to you by your imagination. Let them remind you of your absolute right to free exploration and expression in your writing and in your life. Perhaps you might put this sign up beside the place where you write. Or you might make a card and carry it around and look at it when the presence of the thought patrol feels near. You might even let it become your mantra and chant it from time to time, but please do not forget it. Permission is granted because you are alive. This fact alone is its source. It is the reason I say everything is always permitted in the imagination.

This chapter began with lines from a poem found in Robert Duncan's book *The Opening of the Field*. I'd like to conclude with the closing lines of this poem because within them the nature of our imagination is so beautifully confirmed.

> *Often I am permitted to return to a meadow*
> *as if it were a given property of the mind*
> *that certain bounds hold against chaos,*
>
> *that is a place of first permission,*
> *everlasting omen of what is.*

HOW TO FEED
A HUNGRY GHOST

☾

There is an apocryphal tale about Saint Francis of Assisi that is a sort of ghost story. When I first heard it, the significance of the tale rang so immediately true to my own life, and to the personal and creative lives of friends, that I felt an urgency to tell it to everyone I could. In each case, when I was through relating it, the person with whom I had been speaking smiled with a look of recognition that only experience can bring, as if to say, "It's really true."

Most people have heard that Saint Francis was a great friend of the natural world. You may even have seen images of him that show the intimate connection with nature he so clearly felt as part of who he was. But despite the feeling of empathy with which he approached all living things, it turns out there was one form of life the man who would become known as Saint Francis just could not abide: lepers. It may be shocking to hear this, but when Francis was a young man, even his great heart could not form a bridge to the men and women who suffered from this terrible disease.

The young friar considered this a great moral failing, of course, and he did not take this failing lightly. He knew that the power of his revulsion and fear was causing him to reject people who in all other ways were just like him, except for the misfortune of having been afflicted in this particular way. But try as he might, Francis was unable to get to the root of his feelings and overcome them. Every time the thought of lepers or leprosy crossed his mind, he felt so overcome that his natural goodness seemed instantly consumed by a kind of internal ghost whose hunger devoured his love for life. It even attacked his religious conviction to serve all of God's creatures and ate away at the loving nature of his own heart.

As time passed, Francis cultivated those ways of living that helped to increase the depth of his spiritual understanding. His compassion for all other forms of life increased, and his every move seemed inspired by his boundless love of the Divine. But the secret knowledge of his feelings about lepers preyed upon Francis deeply and undermined his belief in himself in one matter after another. Of course, this was the working of the hungry ghost. Day and night Francis felt the demands of its appetite as it roamed freely within his conscience and imagination. It gnawed at him. It prevented him from sleeping and taking food. It depleted his ability to concentrate in prayer. It stirred up so many seeds of self-hatred and doubt that Francis became convinced he was a sham. He accused himself of insincerely playing the part of one who loves God's world, and this one thought shook him to the root.

Finally, feeling almost completely consumed by this demon-ghost, Francis knew he was incapable of withstanding the attack one more day. He rose from his sickbed and went to see his spiritual friend, to whom he confessed his dilemma. Then he asked his friend for help. Francis's friend was a very wise person who had at one time suffered quite deeply in a similar way. After hearing the depth of Francis's agony and regret, he simply told him, "Francis, just do your best to work this out. The boundless love of Jesus is our guide, and right now, wide as your own heart is, you are being challenged to expand it even more."

"I know," said Francis. "But, as you can see, there is almost nothing left of me. What shall I do?"

His friend looked at him with compassion and then said in a voice so subtle and quiet that Francis could barely hear, "What, indeed!"

Francis left the interview devastated by this reply, and angered at being tossed right back into the very teeth of the devouring mouth. But he also knew that what his friend had said to him was true. That night, during his meditations and prayers, he became determined to conquer this adversarial ghost.

In the morning Francis awakened early, took a bit of nourishment, and resumed his ritual practices as part of the community in which he lived. By midmorning, though he was feeling quite weak, he found himself walking down the dirt path toward the village. It was a beautiful day all around, capped by an unblemished, blue Tuscan sky. Wherever Francis looked every molecule of creation reminded him of the perfection found in all things. This opened his heart, and Francis suddenly recalled that one of the mystical meanings of being born in God's image is that since God is perfect, each of us must be perfect as well, despite what appearances imply.

As Francis walked along the path, contemplating this very thought, a man suddenly stumbled out of the thorn-ridden bushes Francis was about to pass. With one startled look, Francis saw that the man's face was swollen with the deformity of a leper. Without quite knowing what he was doing, Francis leaped at the man, arms outstretched. Then he grabbed the poor man by the shoulders, pulled him so close that they stood breast to breast, and, without the slightest reserve, kissed the leper fully on the mouth. And in that moment, it is said, Francis became Saint Francis, and the leper revealed himself as Christ.

The ability for one person's act to gain a foothold and inspire the life of another is one of the attributes of human truth. Such acts enter the endless body of our own imaginations and dreams. This is part of the mysterious functioning of all authentic expression and art. It is what we want the arts to do. I'm sure you have experienced this after hearing a line of poetry or a musical composition, or sat in wonder as a dancer's gesture inscribed your life upon the air. We just can't turn away from the mirror such expression provides, from what it does inside of us when we recognize that the face beginning to appear in that mirror is our own. This is especially true, because such mirroring leads us to know ourselves in a way that answers our human yearning.

Isn't that what happens when you encounter the undeniable, the true, the real? Don't you often feel that a question has been answered, one you may not even have known you had? I think it is likely that you do. When this occurs, the experience echoes long after the event. It echoes because truth survives. In this case, the truth that cannot be denied is found in the unforgettable echo of a kiss.

Francis's kiss was sufficient to banish the devouring ghost forever. It was a kiss rooted in the desperation to which he had been brought, to be sure, but one also born of the wisdom and courage that drew toward him the embodiment of his greatest fears. In the end, those elements of his psyche that sought to destroy him and those that had to be awakened to keep him alive were not struggling against each other, but *with each other*, in a painful but freeing dance. The kiss was the powerful denouement that set him free.

In our lives the story is not usually so dramatic, though this possibility is not to be denied. Even a seemingly small appetite of this kind has been known to bring the enormity of our lives to a halt. All of a sudden we find ourselves in bed at odd hours, or not eating, or not going to work or seeing friends. We avoid sitting down to write, or nervously circle our meditation pillow one time before we head out of the room. This is what it looks like when our own hungry ghosts become stimulated without warning and begin to eat at us from inside. It is why this tale of Saint Francis is so easily recognized the moment we hear it. It is part of life for almost everyone, and we experience the hunger of these ghosts as real.

Both Eastern and Western religious and secular traditions have had quite a bit to say on the subject of ghosts. One common theme is that the association between ghosts and appetite is quite strong. There might even be an agreement that a ghost *is* appetite personified. In the West, it is believed that ghosts are the spirits of those who were never able to be satisfied when they were alive. Their spirits hang on in some barely transparent form with the hope of attaining some measure of satisfaction at last. Some people are said to be trapped in ghostly form because of the harm they caused during their lifetimes. Their spirits were left so unsettled that they continue to suffer long after their final breaths. These ghosts want to make amends and redeem themselves, but until this yearning is satisfied their haunted presence remains.

Another group of ghosts are the noisy kind. They stay within shouting distance, so to speak, because of what others have done to them. Their appetite is for setting things right as well, but their method is to get even with those who have wronged them. These are the horror-movie ghosts I prefer not to pay to see.

Buddhism speaks about ghosts in a somewhat different way, though their main attribute is still their appetite. In Buddhist cosmology, ghosts are found among the realms of existence known as the Six Realms. These are the realms of Hell, of Hungry Ghosts, of Animals, of Human Beings, of Demigods and Demigoddesses, and of Gods and Goddesses themselves. It is said that our actions produce a certain momentum that propels us into one of these realms or another. This is a simplified description of the workings of karma, a word whose usage these days is found almost everywhere in the West. For those who believe that reincarnation is a constantly upward progression of the soul's refinement, it is fairly easy to understand this list of six realms as a linear sequence where, with any good fortune, conditions make it possible for a life essence or soul to rise fairly rapidly from the realm of Hell to the realm of the Gods and Goddesses in a sort of straight line, with relatively brief, almost touristic stints among the uncomfortable dwellers of the intervening realms. (Actually, despite the seeming desirability of being counted among the gods, traditional Buddhist thought considers the human realm the most precious of all because only human beings have the ability to become enlightened and free from the cycle, or wheel, of suffering.)

Another view sees these six realms as ever-existing places, or existential spots, in which we might find ourselves living in the future. Where we next appear is determined entirely by what we do in the realm where we currently make our home. Therefore, if we do well in the realm of the Animals, in our next life we may move on to the realm of human existence. But if in our human life we get caught by our various weaknesses, attachments, and drives, we get demoted, so to speak, and may spend our next life among the animals (which many of us find somewhat attractive) or the hungry ghosts, or even in hell.

My own sense is that all six realms simultaneously

coexist as potential states of mind within each of us. When the conditions exist that nourish the attributes of one realm more strongly than all the others, that realm takes precedence as the one that most powerfully influences our thinking, feeling, and behavior. So we may be solid, moral citizens of the world at one o'clock in the afternoon, and *one second later* we may find we have leapfrogged into the realm of the Gods or Animals, or that we are simply living with our brothers and sisters in Hell. If you give it a little thought, you might see what I mean. For example, how has your day or your weekend gone thus far? Good? Not so good? And what have you been feeling? How have you responded to what has presented itself today? In just how many realms have you been?

Saint Francis was afflicted by a hungry, hungry ghost. Despite the avidity of its appetite in this story, it remains the kind of ghost most of us encounter every day. Buddhist iconography imagines these hungry ghosts, called *preta* in Sanskrit, in a way I find memorably descriptive. They are beings with huge bellies that serve as storehouses for all they can possibly consume, but their throats are as narrow as the needle you use to sew a patch on your clothes. Because of this conflict, no matter how much they place into their mouths, they can never be satisfied. This is precisely why they perpetually devour anything they can get.

So, what are our hungry ghosts, our *preta?* What part of ourselves rises from the depths of our own psyche and drives the needs of its appetite into our daily lives? Who is willing to consume anything in its path without regard to what may be damaged or destroyed? Of course, for each of us the answer will be different, and you may find it useful to spend some time asking such questions. If you do, please do so gently, with the simple desire to understand what makes you behave the way you do in both your inner and outer world. Any other approach means your inquiry is in the hands of a hungry ghost. I suggest that you focus particular attention on the various hungry ghosts that seek to interrupt the expression of your creative and spiritual life. These ghosts serve a master whose needs are relentlessly demanding and, as I mentioned, insatiable at the core, so their methods can be deceptively sly.

If you recall what happened to Saint Francis, I think you'll find a good starting place. He was beset by his greatest unspoken fear. If you could name your own unspoken fears in regard to your creative life, what would you say? Perhaps you might believe that you really can't do it—that you can't write well, or at least well enough to express what most wants to be said. Perhaps you fear that, in truth, you have nothing of interest, nothing deep or wise enough, to say.

These types of fears are common to most artists and writers I know. But they are also very useful fears. While they do cause the creative tension that drives us crazy with insecurity and doubt, they also provide the energy necessary to go where we have to go, to get said what must be said. It is a dual-edged tension many artists consider an unavoidably necessary part of the creative process itself. Remember how essential to Saint Francis's breakthrough his desperation really was and you will see what I mean.

If this energizing, maddening tension finds itself in the hands of the hungry ghost who serves the part of the ego that fears what you might discover or create, the situation can get very serious very fast. The awakening of this particular appetite can bring forth behaviors of a quite destructive nature. It can unbalance the creative tension and turn it into an unreasonable irritability or anger that friends and partners find hard to withstand. It can transform this unbalance into self-hatred. It can engender nightmares that leave us shaking with insecurity. It can enforce a monumental wasting of time during our supposed work hours, which eventually eats away at our confidence and self-esteem. I've seen this self-destructive domino effect happen to people again and again. Remember how Francis's fear set off a chain reaction within his body and mind? It is easily done.

Sometimes, in order to satisfy their appetite, the sleight of hand these hungry ghosts use might appear friendly. How many times have you set aside an hour, or a day, or a week, or made arrangements to go on a retreat to do your creative or spiritual work, only to come back with much less than you had planned to accomplish? And how often has this caused you to doubt your sincerity and skill? How many times have the very things you've set in motion to help you express your deepest self seemingly been turned against you? When expectations find themselves in the toolbox of a hungry ghost, all I can say is *"Watch Out!"*

There are countless examples I could offer, but one I do want to highlight is so unnerving, and so common, it is worth going into. It occurs when our writing is going well. In this circumstance the shakiness of the destructive part of our ego, and therefore the appetite of the ghost, grows larger with every authentic word. The attention we give to our work during such times leaves this hungry part of ourselves feeling neglected. It realizes we have found a genuine way to express the depths of our lives and considers this a very threatening situation. *What about me?* becomes its mantra. Since its own continuity appears at stake, it seeks to protect itself with a move so subtle that I can only admire its creative reserve.

It tests us with a sotto voce approach by allowing us a feeling of self-satisfaction. Not so bad, all in all, except that it simultaneously plants within hearing distance of our conscious mind the seed that perhaps this satisfaction may not really be deserved if looked at closely. In other words, we feel a certain amount of pride for the day's work and may even allow ourselves a sigh of true satisfaction, but because we suspect that what we feel may be a bit too much, at the end of that sigh we experience a flutter of doubt. These are ghost tricks.

Once both elements of this move are in place, the ghost begins to inflate us. It tells us we are really great. It may even mirror its own feeling of neglect and begin to argue that others are not as good as we are; that we deserve a kind of recognition we have not yet received. If this maneuver catches us unaware, it is bad news indeed. Feelings of grandiosity are often the flip side of low self-esteem, and once we become caught in this particular web, the hungry ghost has succeeded. It has enmeshed us in a sort of psychic seesaw where no matter which seat we are on, our situation is not so good.

It may seem impossible to defeat such an internal process as the hungry ghost. This was the source of Saint Francis's rage when his friend answered, "What, indeed!" You may find yourself thinking, *What? Another hundred years of therapy?* And I agree with you. The idea of battling a common and, some may argue, natural process of the human psyche makes no sense to me. We do not have to defeat ourselves. We do not have to hate any part of ourselves. To engage in such a confrontation is itself a trick of the hungry ghost. Then it will really control the energy and attention we need to bring to other parts of our lives.

Rather than engaging them in terms they would find beneficial, we can understand the functioning of these hungry ghosts well enough to actually feed them, but in a manner that frees us from their control. In this way we are taking care of them while healthily assisting those parts of ourselves that give rise to such hunger in the first place. It is a life-giving action, an expression of love applied to ourselves, and it works out well in the end.

Once you have used the method I've learned for taking care of hungry ghosts, I hope you will agree that it is simple, wise, and effective. There is even a certain elegance of mind to it you may enjoy. It comes from the Zen practice of eating the lunchtime meal in a ritualized, formal style called *oryoki* in Japanese. Without going into an extensive description of this beautiful and meaningful spiritual practice, I'd like to offer a brief definition of *oryoki:* "just the right amount." When we learn how to prepare food, how to serve and how to receive it, how to eat, and how to live "just the right amount," we can apply it to our relationships, our creative work, our hungry ghosts, and to every aspect of our lives.

At a certain point during the meal, all of the participants

put down their utensils and take a small pinch of food, sometimes as small as one grain of rice, from the first of the three
bowls before them. This bowl, which rests on the left side of
the eating mat, is the largest of the three. It is known as the
Buddha bowl, and therefore it is said to contain the food of
awakening within it. The bit of food is grasped between the
thumb and index finger and placed on the end of a utensil
very much like a small spatula, which will be used to clean the
bowls after the meal. All of this traditionally takes place right
at the mat where the person meditates, eats, and sometimes
sleeps. As the participants do this the leader chants the following words:

> All evil spirits, now I give you this offering.
> This food will pervade everywhere.

This ritual is sometimes known as the Feeding of the
Hungry Ghosts, and it is these ghosts that are referred to by
the words *evil spirits*. Please note that despite these ghosts'
identification as "evil," they are fed directly from the Buddha's
bowl, from the food of awakening. I am sure you will recognize right away the wisdom in this. If we offer the food of
awakening to a part of ourselves that is lost, it has a chance to
realize something it needs very badly.

I started to approach my own hungry ghosts in this way
many years ago, after first encountering this practice, and I
have developed various ways to practice feeding my hungry
ghosts even when I am not eating an *oryoki* meal. It actually
makes me happy when I do it. Rather than becoming invested

in the distracting drama they provide to pull me away from what I've set out to do, I take care of them. Let me suggest that you, too, can take care of your own hungry ghosts by ritualizing a way of feeding them just the right amount. What would that look like in practical terms? One technique that has proven to work well is done every day as you sit down to write. All that is needed is for you to jot down just one phrase of poetry, or even just one word that calls forth an image you really love. Some people prefer to write a word symbolic of a spiritual teaching that expresses their aspirations. Remember, whatever you write can be the symbolic size, and carry the symbolic significance, of one grain of rice. This means your offering can be small and big at the same time. The most important thing is for you to make your offering with the same kind of mind that Zen practitioners have when they place that single grain of rice upon the cleaning stick. Do it with the intention of acknowledging your hungry ghosts and feeding them the very best of foods. Then, if you like, place the paper with the writing you have done into a beautiful bowl beside the area where you write.

Of course, this is only one possible design for your ritual feeding of the hungry ghosts, and it may work for you, or it may not be a perfect fit. In the latter case, I do hope you enjoy finding a way to give something to your hungry ghosts with the intention of satisfying them. Lighting a candle or a stick of incense works well. Closing your eyes, breathing quietly for a moment, and telling yourself *I am here* works as well. The techniques you can devise are countless. They are opportunities for you to enjoy your creativity in ways that may be entirely new. The most important part of this ritual, however, is the spirit and continuity with which you carry it out. Done in the right spirit every day before you write, it is an offering, a practice, well worth doing.

After you have performed this part of your ritual, there is one more thing you need to do for it to be complete. If you find that as you work—or later in the day, after you have written—the hungry ghosts appear with their appetite in full disorder, offer them a generous and gentle smile of recognition that lights up their world as the most delicious of foods, and tell them, *I fed you today. You've already eaten.* Then, without a second's thought, go back to what you were doing. And I mean *without a second's thought!* This will remind them, and you, that they have been fed and will receive no further attention or consideration than that. With just a little sincere and consistent practice on your part, I know you will find how effective this really is. Even the most insistent intruder will vanish.

I have tried to write the tale of Saint Francis and the teaching on feeding the hungry ghost in a voice that encompasses both the severity of our human dilemma and the lightness and wisdom of an approach that can help us to set ourselves free. We don't have to meet big guns with big guns. A little real understanding of what we face, and a commitment to act based on that understanding, goes a long way.

I'd like to leave you with these thoughts. Once you have performed some ritual gesture to feed the hungry ghosts, the simple act of reminding them that they have already eaten is a very powerful and yet gentle form of Francis's kiss. Just as it was necessary for him to withdraw his projections and fears before he could realize his true self, feeding our hungry ghosts is a necessary part of our own process of becoming who we really are. The physical, emotional, psychological, spiritual, and creative energy we've used in the past to battle these hungry ghosts becomes released by these simple but skillful means. It is transformed into a wellspring. Then, when it is time for us to draw from the clarified depth of our own real self, the true nature of our being will spontaneously emerge.

THE NARROW PLACE

☾

Though I take my song from a withered limb,
both song and tree they sing for Him.

—LEONARD COHEN

I have always loved the Jewish holiday Passover, which cele-
brates the Exodus of the Jews from ancient Egypt. In its
largest sense it acknowledges the yearning and struggle for
freedom common to all people. I find that the symbols and
teachings of this holiday are ripe with inspiration. I suspect,
however, my real love for this day began when I learned that
my Hebrew name, *Pesach,* was also the word for Passover.

As a young boy I held the story of the Exodus fully in
my imagination, and I would say this name to myself over and
over again as the holiday drew near. With each mantralike rep-

etition I would feel the powerful story of the name moving through me. *Pesach!* I would say, feeling the stones of Egypt crushing my back. *Pesach!* and I would paint lamb's blood over the lintel of my imagined doorway so the Angel of Death would pass over the house and not kill the firstborn son. Then it would be *Pesach!* for the breathlike sound of the Angel's wings as they passed above us, the breath of life. *Pesach!* for those who lived as slaves in *Mitzrayim,* "the narrow place," the Hebrew word for Egypt. And *Pesach!* for the spirit of the people who longed to be free. *Pesach!* for Moses, who led them to the edge of the Red Sea, and *Pesach!* for the miracle of its waters parting. *Pesach!* I would say, for the faith that let our people cross over to the promised land. And *Pesach!* for all such stepping across, for all such miracles, for all people.

The story, the name, the urgency spoke so eloquently to my imagination, I could barely hold it all inside. As I grew, and came into contact with more extensive interpretations, I realized that the reach of this story was limitless; that the very rituals reenacting the story every year at Passover tables throughout the world extended the message beyond my family, beyond my tribe, to everyone. After all, who does not want to be free?

There are several obligations that must be performed at every Passover meal, or seder. One is that the children must be taught the story. Every year, teaching the story to the children is a wonderful opportunity for adults to notice how their own understanding has grown. A second obligation is the central focus of this chapter. As I mentioned above, the Hebrew word for Egypt is *Mitzrayim,* "the narrow place." At first hearing,

Mitzrayim may sound like it refers solely to Egypt, the land ruled by Pharaoh, where the Jews' lives were narrowed to the status of slaves. But it is more than that. At each seder people are asked to spend a few moments contemplating how they have related to the narrow place in their own lives during that year. The narrow place may be defined as the ways in which others have constrained our lives, or it may be seen as how we have enslaved ourselves, causing a narrowing of hope, possibility, expression. We might even look into whether we are helping the deepest part of ourselves to fulfill its potential. Ultimately, our exploration of how we relate to the narrow place reveals where we are on our own path to freedom.

This obligation exists so that we may remain conscious and choose to nourish the needs of our true selves, including our relationship to the Divine. Sometimes, what we see may look pretty good; there may be signs of progress since the previous year. At other times we may notice places where improvements can be made. To satisfy this obligation by reflecting deeply strengthens our aspiration to find the path to freedom for ourselves and others in the world.

I want to tell two stories that mirror our human freedom where some form of constriction or enslavement might well have taken place. I offer them here as a form of gratitude for the vision they contain, and to inspire you in your relationship with *Mitzrayim*.

The first concerns a day when I was standing on the boardwalk across from the Pacific Ocean in Venice, California, with my friend Tom, a photographer with an extraordinary eye. We had just come out of Tom's studio and were watching as the sky took on the spacious quality of twilight blue that sometimes comes as a gift to this part of the world. As if this wasn't enough, it was one of those days when the particulates of desert air had traveled westward from the distant Mojave and turned the dying sun into a classic red lantern resting on the horizon's edge.

As we stood there, watching the sun's descent, we noticed that a man leaning on a three-pronged walker was slowly making his way further up the strand. His route caused him to be momentarily backlit by the sun, which turned the shape his body made as he leaned on his walker into a silhouette. As soon as we saw the concentrated gesture of his steps we recognized the man as someone local to the Venice boardwalk scene. I don't know the details of his personal story, but in the end he was left lifting one foot after another in a slow and painful manner, assisted by the walker that he held in an awkwardly turned hand. The entire process required a delicate balance not easy to achieve. As I looked at him, I noticed that the effort required by each step was so demanding it propelled his body forward with a slight lurch that caused the length of his ponytail to skip a little, as if by surprise, into the air. *Such seeming whimsy created by such pain,* I thought. And yet, there was a surprising if ungainly fluidity of rhythm and grace to this man's movements that mysteriously added a sense of spaciousness to the air.

Tom and I watched in silence, with an appreciation and respect for the integrity this man brought to every step as his figure faded into shadow and the sun dispersed its light a little further across the sea. Then Tom turned to me and said in his thoughtful way, "Whenever I see him I feel like I'm watching the most beautiful and rarest of cranes."

Sometime later Tom called to tell me the following story. It seems there is a ritual of sorts that occurs whenever Itzhak Perlman gives a concert on his violin. Due to being stricken with polio at the age of four, he walks with a slow and awkward gait, assisted by braces on both legs and crutches. It is an effort for him to make his way onto the stage, and his entry often strikes a chord with the audience. They feel gratitude for the integrity of spirit he so clearly expresses through his presence—and, of course, for the beauty of his music.

According to Tom's account of the night in question, after Perlman had made his painstaking entrance across the stage, he proceeded to seat himself in his usual and somewhat ritualistic way. This required a careful placing of his crutches on the floor and a releasing of the clasps that lock the leg braces in place. Each motion took him, and his audience, closer to the composition he would play, but there was an attentive and gentle rhythmic concentration in these gestures as well. After this prelude, the master violinist slowly arranged his legs and feet in a posture that allowed for some measure of comfort before lifting his bow and his violin, which he settled in position beneath his chin. Then, with the slightest of nods offered to the waiting conductor, the music began.

But on this particular night something unexpected took place just after Perlman began to play. He was not more than one minute into the music, playing beautifully with his eyes closed and his bow floating across the strings, when an unmistakable sound was heard throughout the concert hall. One of his violin strings had snapped. The conductor brought the orchestra to a halt, but the kind of nervous titter that at other times might accompany such a moment was in no way present in the auditorium. The thought that Perlman might have to rise from his seat, go through the ritual of reestablishing his ability to stand, and then walk off the stage to replace the broken string was clearly on everyone's mind. It could be heard in the audience's collective silence, as if each person was refusing to exhale until the next move was revealed.

Perlman sighed the briefest of sighs, though there was also a bit of a smile on his face as he inspected the broken string. Then he replaced his violin beneath his chin, nodded again in the direction of the conductor, closed his eyes, and continued to play. And how he played! It was as if he would make the world new again; and if he could no longer use four strings, then he would use three to repair its wounds and return it to a wholeness it needed more than ever before.

The passion and tonal purity that poured out of Perlman's violin made it clear that he had entered into a relationship with himself, the music, the composer, and perhaps even with the source of life itself; one he may not have previously known. On and on, as the concerto progressed, he played with a startling freedom. Each movement of his bow took him to some further place beneath the music as he seemingly reconfigured the composition with a spontaneity and drive that required his fingers to be new fingers, his strings to be new strings. Out of this imperfect moment, Perlman was creating a purity of musical expression that was stunning to behold. And then it was over. That is, except for the wild pounding and shouting of the audience.

When the audience's appreciation finally died down, Perlman smiled again, as he had earlier that night just before taking up the bow for the second time. Then he spoke, clearly tired from the effort of his extraordinary playing, but with a modesty that in its own way made possible the triumph of what he had just done. "Sometimes," he said, with a generosity of spirit that defines the man, "you must find out how much music you can make with what you have left." And then, slowly, to a tumultuous response, he placed his violin down, rose from his chair, and walked in the only way he could from the stage.

The musical brilliance and wisdom Perlman offered on this night of nights, and the ungainly yet graceful sunset walk of the man in California, speak powerfully of *Mitzrayim,* and the potential for what may be brought to life in such a land. They also remind me of Edmond Jabès, an Egyptian-born Jewish poet who lived and wrote in exile in Paris. When asked if it was still possible to write poetry after the Holocaust, Jabès replied simply, *"One must."*

How truly Perlman's single sentence and Jabès's two words ring in the human heart. Yet, despite the fact that in some of our lives this heart may have prematurely narrowed on the stem of its spirit, in most cases it remains a heart that longs to pick up the bow as Perlman did and make the world whole again, one note at a time.

As we all know, this is not easily done. Sometimes, when

our spirits have been so wounded by life's rigor that it feels difficult to go on, the only word needed to describe the cause of our despair is *life*. How paradoxical this is. But the real danger comes when this narrowing of the courage to move forward in our lives—*coeur*, the root of the word *courage*, means "heart"—turns against the source of life itself. This kind of despair, the archetypal dark night, is exactly what Perlman's musical explosion, and all creative expression, oppose.

The literal and metaphorical ground this counterargument stands upon is clear: The source of life, of creation, is embedded in each molecule and moment of our world. It is the true content and substance of our lives. What is called the Creation is a continuous and ongoing process that we cocreate with all things. The pulse of life is here for us to draw upon, but *we* must lift the bow.

The significance of this is especially salient during times when our lives can only be played on three strings. The narrow place that I spoke of earlier is not just the artery where the Angel of Death resides, but the necessary birth channel through which life must pass on its way to full expression in the world. It can be here that our deepest selves come alive.

During a period in my life when the narrow place was all I could feel, I made it my practice, several times a week, to go to a certain spot in the nearby mountains to sit quietly, meditate, and write. In order to be gentle with myself, I decided before going that if I wrote something, that was good, and if I didn't, that was also good. I would benefit from the chance to enjoy the quiet of a beautiful place. More often than not, after I had finished meditating, something would draw my attention away from the constriction I was experiencing and I would write with the same vulnerability I had experienced earlier as pain. Sometimes I would write no more than a few lines. Sometimes it would be a short poem. And at other times several short poems would arrive in one sitting. Ultimately, I made a book of these called *One Hundred Butterflies.* Here are two poems that came within minutes of each other. When I look at them now, I can still feel their significance and mood.

Tall grasses
have much to teach
the bowed head of a man

~

Just when I was feeling lonely
the wind played a little joke
on some leaves

As one week of following this practice led to another, I found it was creating the space I needed in order to breathe again. The walls of *Mitzrayim* were being pushed back, and a renewed desire to engage life was being born. I looked forward to going into the mountains to breathe freely and counteract the "bricking in" that was caused by pain.

When I was finally able to look with some objectivity at what I was doing, I saw that going to the same spot on a consistent basis, and sitting still while engaging the truths of my heart and mind, was a form of discipline very similar to following the guidelines of a spiritual practice. It was the rigors of this discipline that set me back on the path of freedom. Freedom through restraint. Spaciousness through constriction. Having experienced this so powerfully, I was able to write

> *Once inside the bamboo tube*
> *the snake*
> *learns a new way*

In order to begin working with the narrow place of *Mitzrayim*—the constrictions to your own freedom and expression that exist right now in your life—please take out your writing materials, place them to the side of the table where you will write, and sit down. As in every exercise, be sure your workspace is not cluttered. A clear space encourages a clarity of heart and mind. When you are comfortably seated, allow yourself to breathe quietly with your eyes either open or closed until your breathing becomes steady and your body feels relaxed. Then read what follows and begin the exercise.

The Sufi poet Hafiz wrote that our bodies are restless until all the soul's beauty is painted upon the sky. When we give a subtle and careful attention to our bodies, we are able to stay in touch with the experience of our deeper selves. Those who separate the two and denigrate the body as a means of praising the spirit may not be looking deeply enough at the nature of what we are and how it all fits together. Therefore, in order to explore the narrow place, I am going to ask you to use the resource of your body now.

With your eyes closed, sense your body's experience of itself at this moment. If you like, you can gently scan yourself from head to toe to discover any places where you feel knotted up. You don't have to do anything about these places now except to notice them. When you feel ready, let your attention settle in the area of your heart. Then, after a few moments of focusing, say the words *Mitzrayim* or *the narrow place* just one time. It doesn't matter which of these you choose, as long as you allow yourself to feel when you say the words. After you do, take a deep breath. As you slowly exhale, notice how you respond in your body or imagination. Be sure to observe any images that flash through your mind, any thoughts or memories. Be aware of your bodily sensations and the emotional response you have as well.

One participant in a workshop reported that when she did this first part of the exercise a shudder ran through her because she was spontaneously reminded of the loss of her father at an early age. She thought she had made peace with this sad fact years before, and so the memory took her completely by surprise. She had never before realized how profoundly this loss had robbed her of hope, how specifically it had taken away her own belief in freedom. "And why the shudder?" I asked. "Why not a shout or cry?" She thought about this for a moment and said, "As soon as I focused on my heart and said '*the narrow place*' I made the connection. My father's face came out of the dark, and I heard myself say, 'I'll never be free.' It was like being struck by lightning. My body felt electrified with pain." The writing this woman did at the end of the exercise poignantly explored the trinity of lightning, her father's death, and her belief that she would never know a moment of freedom in her life.

This is only one fairly provocative example of what can occur when you give yourself fully to this exercise. Of course, each person responds in a way most truly his own: While some responses may be quite striking and dramatic, others will be more subtle, like a thought or a feeling just taking form. For this reason, if it feels important to do so, I encourage you to repeat this process several times to experience your responses as deeply as possible. Work with this in a way that makes sense to you. Shape it to your need to know the truth of the narrow place as you experience it in the area of your heart. Afterward, write down your responses and imagery fully, exploring any avenue that opens up to you, and then prepare to move on.

When you feel ready to continue, please return to an awareness of your breathing while establishing a gently concentrated mind. Give yourself a minute or so to do this. Now move your attention to the area around your belly that rises and falls on the rhythm of your breath. Place your awareness here and settle in until you feel fully present. When you do, repeat the process of saying either *Mitzrayim* or *the narrow place*. You may be quite surprised to note how different your responses are from the ones you experienced when you focused on your heart. Different parts of the body tend to produce different feelings, distinct imagery. Repeat this part of the exercise, focusing solely on the area around your belly, until you have fully experienced your responses. When you have, be sure to give yourself as much time as you need to write. Of course, you may always use this or any part of the exercise as a resource for future writing, but the spirit of risk and permission is so alive right now that I hope you will explore what you have just experienced as deeply as you can.

After you have completed this second part of the exercise, you may want to move on, or you may want to take a short break. Of course, taking a breather is fine. As you can see, there is a pacing inherent in performing each part of the exercise. This pacing is an important part of the unique creative process each of us possesses and must be respected. When you follow your own pace, you nourish the needs of your deeper self and encourage it to give you more of what you need.

To complete this exercise, we are going to repeat this procedure three more times. First, your point of focus will be your throat. Remember to begin by establishing a steady pattern of breath and then, when the focus of attention on your throat is calm and clear, go through the process of saying *Mitzrayim* or *the narrow place*. Having noticed all of the responses this calls forth, be sure to give yourself enough time to write fully at the end.

After you have completed this, bring your awareness to your genital area. As with the other regions, this part of your body retains an enormous amount of information and experience that will be released as you do the exercise with a quiet, listening mind. Be sure to give full voice to whatever comes from focusing here.

The last exploration is done a bit differently. Please lean

on the table by planting your elbows firmly before you, place your head in your hands, breathe quietly, and say *Mitzrayim* or *the narrow place* deeply into your mind. Do this several times. Afterward, let yourself feel any of your responses for as long as you like and then begin to write.

You have just completed a large amount of spiritual, emotional, and creative work. Given the central position the narrow place holds in most of our lives, the writing this exercise calls forth can be quite powerful, and so I urge you to read slowly through what you have written. Of course, when approached with a serious intent, this exercise can take quite a bit out of us, but it can also provide an enormous amount of energy. Our spirits grow light and give off a radiance when we give voice to what has kept them narrow and dark, constricted and afraid. Many students have used this exercise and the internal work it demands to generate a considerable amount of writing. Some have even worked for years on realizations and connections that this exercise brought about. Please feel free to come back to this work whenever you can to discover what else it holds.

The final exercise based on the narrow place will take some planning. In order to receive the greatest benefit from the teachings in this chapter, I urge you to take it up as soon as you can. Just as I made a practice of going into the mountains to engage the narrow place and to allow my contact with the world to help create the spaciousness I needed, I'd like you to make a commitment of the same order. Find a place you want to visit repeatedly, where you will be able to hear and think and feel, and commit to going there to write at least once a week. Your commitment should be for no less than four weeks. It really does not matter if you live in the country or in the city; while the place you choose is important, it is not as crucial as the consistency with which you go there and the quality of concentration you give to yourself and your work once you are there. I have written as authentically in the heart of the New York Public Library on Forty-second Street in New York City, with many people bustling around me, as I have while sitting alone on a mountain on the island of Hokkaido, in Japan.

When Matisse would go into the natural world to paint, he would draw an outline around his feet right there on the ground. He did this so he could re-place himself in the exact spot when he returned later on to complete the painting. This gave his perspective a fixed point. It allowed him to notice with precision what was different in the landscape, and what had remained the same. This approach is quite similar to developing a simple but consistent spiritual practice. It also provides a great benefit for us as writers.

We need a fixed point, a point of constant reference, in order to notice the shape and changes of our minds. The frightened part of our egos will argue against such a practice and try to convince us that it is constraining, that it restricts our freedom, that it isn't natural. But if you look carefully at how nature really works you will see how much of its life and beauty depend upon consistency and the repetition of particular patterns in order to live and grow. Without certain fixed points in our own lives, we may become like a bird that flies around and around in a treeless land without knowing where to set down. As human beings in a modern world, we may get exhausted, lose the quality of our attention, or ignore the proper relationships we need to sustain us. Then we may make a mistake that can cost something very dear to us, even our own lives.

After you go to the spot you have chosen and settle in, take notice of what is happening in the world directly around you. If you are in a natural setting, notice simple things like the movement of the grasses, or the leaves. Take a look at what forms the shadows make. Notice what the insects or lizards or frogs may be doing right then. Observe the relationships between things. If you are in the city, do the same. Notice what life is doing all around you.

When you have engaged your self and the world in this way, notice how the narrowing in your life can be symbolized by what you see. Allow the shapes and forms of life to become metaphors for the narrow place or, with equal power, for the freedom from narrowness you seek. Be sure to write all of this down and make a commitment to develop immediately any image that calls to you. You might observe how the narrow place and some grasses have a conversation, as I did in my earlier poem. It was so personally moving to see how first the wind bowed them down, and how each time they were able to lift again. Another of the *Butterfly* poems says

> *First wind blows leaves*
> *out of the tree*
> *then it teaches them to dance*

Once again, the action of the wind and leaves was so ordinary, yet by setting out to see nature's way as symbolic of my life, and by following through on my commitment to write it down, I was able to understand my suffering in a way that also released a vision of joy.

I hope you will give this approach a chance. If you are in the city, carefully sense the feeling inside you as you observe someone walking nearby. Remember my friend Tom's observation about "the most beautiful and rarest of cranes" as we watched the man walk with a painful grace along the strand. He reminded me to always look for beauty, and I have returned to this theme again and again because it rises from the authentic ground of my being. It is so important to look for details of this order and for the connections and possibilities that the slightest gesture suggests to your imagination.

Why not dedicate the first half hour of each week's visit to making a list of such details to use in your writing. I think of this as gathering seeds. It helps you to develop the kind of quiet concentration upon which writing and all creative expression depends. It sharpens your eye, connects you to your environment, activates your imagination, and gets you writing from the start. The grip of a hand upon a cane or the sudden dance of light on darkened ground can speak as powerful metaphors for our own lives. Gather these seeds and give yourself to the details with care. Then find the images that truly rise from your own authentic ground and begin to write.

As you go each week to your given spot and gather images and connections, I am sure you will find that there are many ways your inner world and the world in which you have placed yourself intersect. Give yourself permission to perceive and make any associations you need for true expression to occur. Then write for as long as you like with this permission as an unwavering ally. Remember, when you give the narrow place an opportunity to be expressed, you help create a path of freedom, a path you can follow into every part of your life.

A NEED TO KNOW

(

Love is dead in us
if we forget
the virtues of an amulet
and quick surprise.
—ROBERT CREELEY

Often when we work deeply in the narrow place, profound, sometimes uncomfortable questions arise. After all, we are exploring some of the most significant questions of all: What and where is our path to freedom? Because of the poignancy of the situation, many smaller questions may arise like quick surprises from the depths of our imagination. If we stop to consider them and seek out their hidden meaning, they can serve as powerful catalysts in our lives. Frequently, questions appear in our minds accompanied by a particular feeling of lucidity—an experience of precise knowing—even if we cannot articulate what we suddenly understand. It is as if these are not questions at all, but cleverly disguised answers. In this regard such questions behave like poignant images that bring a feeling of resolution, a sense of clarity and peace. If we are receptive to the subtle details that make these questions what they are, their poetic and spiritual insight may help to shape meaning in our lives. After all, we are the weavers who fabricate these questions; they are intended solely for us.

A number of years ago, after helping to bury my friend Michael, who died in his forties without any sign of prior illness, I walked to my car feeling wrapped in a great cloud of emptiness that paradoxically held me at its center. Those of us who had been close to him not only felt a great measure of sorrow at our loss but were shocked as well, and I noticed that when we caught one another's eyes during the service, we could only shake our heads in wonder at the meaning of a friend's life cut so tragically short.

In my own case, the suddenness of Michael's death left a bit too much space in the area surrounding my heart. It even seemed that my heart had become more tenuous, like an unanswered question suspended in air. But this was not the only thing that appeared transformed. The world without my friend looked different to me. The leaves on the trees as I walked from the chapel and the sparkling mica embedded in the black pitch of the road seemed to have been made new by loss. I saw them from a distance, as if they were part of some strange world. *What is a leaf?* I thought. *What is a road? Why are any of us here?*

To seek the origin of any life is to seek the source of life itself. This is why it is crucial for us to greet questions such as the ones above with a willingness to follow where they want to lead. In many cases, a question may serve as the proverbial finger pointing at the moon. But questions can do more than just point in the direction of an insight our psyche wants us to discover. They can serve as spiritual teachings in themselves. They can be the moon calling us to join them there, which we know how to do. To embrace a question born in our imagination is to feel embraced. It is no different from the embrace we may feel in the midst of a forest or a dream. We should give ourselves over completely with the same open disposition all creativity requires.

Since questions are not just random thoughts, but derive from the needs of our deepest self, I think of them as invitations to dance. Something wonderful can happen when we say yes. But questions have a persistent nature, and if we don't answer them, they will often seek other ways to gain our attention. They may call to us during our waking hours and then appear again in our dreams when there is something we really need to know. If we still do not heed them, it is not uncommon for an illness to stop our lives until we hear what our questions have to say.

Sometimes the question is a kind of early warning system that subtly communicates *Don't!* or *Yes!* Sometimes it is a matter of survival. From the very beginning of our lives we have a relationship with questions that is based on need. Our infant eyes scan whatever is before us, wondering, *What is that? Who's there? Do I know it? Like it? Hate it? Does it hold that something that fills my belly? Is it warm?* Even at this early stage of awareness, we begin to identify our deepest needs and desires through questions. But as we grow and find that we can't quite put our finger on the question anymore, or the means to express it, life can become difficult. If we become diverted and end up asking a question that might not really address our deepest needs, things can go badly indeed.

The tragedy of Hamlet is a perfect example of this. Faced with the murder of his father and the betrayal by his mother and her new husband, the young prince suffers terribly. In his famous soliloquy of indecisive grief and despair, Hamlet declares: *"To be or not to be, that is the question."* It is perhaps the most well-known moment of the play. But it is not the question. The question for Hamlet is contained in the very first words of the play: *"Who's there?"* This is shouted into the night by the sentry who sees Banquo's ghost. *"Who's there?"*

If Hamlet had been able to ask this question of himself, the tragedy might not have played out as it did. *"To be or not to be"* is not the question. Hamlet *is*. But *who is he?* Who or what are we? That is the question. It is the very question that lies at the root of our lives.

In the book of Exodus, when the Infinite spoke to Moses out of the bush that burned but was not consumed—which I take to be a natural symbol of the creative source of life—we are told that Moses asks, *"Who am I that I should lead the people out of Egypt?"* It is a question of pure humility and truth. It may appear that Moses was asking this solely of God, but questions of this order are always part of the internal dialogue we have with our deepest selves, and so we should not overlook the probability that Moses was listening for an answer from inside himself as well. Shortly afterward, when Moses asks what he should say to the Israelites if they ask the name of the one who has sent him, he hears the words *"I am That I am. Tell them* I am *has sent you."* Name and being as one.

One interpretation of this remarkable moment is that in addition to declaring his sovereignty, God sought to awaken the imagination of the man who stood before him so that he, too, might find the way to unify being and name. After all, according to the tradition, God knows what demands will be placed on the man who will lead a people to freedom. He knows what continued strength and wisdom will be required. He also knows that in order for spiritual maturity to develop in the human realm, the answer to the question *Who am I?* must be the powerful but humble declaration *I am!*

In one teaching from mystical Judaism we are told that between birth and the age of forty we ask *Why?* This question is found all through the play *Hamlet,* and it is a perfect question for us to ask when we are young. In part it reflects our curiosity about the world, but it also arises from an understandable lack of self-knowledge and a feeling of not being able to really influence the world we have received. But after we are grown, the nature of the question must change. It becomes *Who? Who am I? Who is here? Who is this one that lives?* Once this question is engaged all other questions are found within its limitless grounds.

Questions of a deep nature are at the root of every wisdom tradition. Sometimes I think the question, all on its own, *is* a wisdom tradition. One of the reasons for their prominence is that even when we have no intuition about where they may lead, questions rooted in our need to know have an authenticity that is unmistakable. It is this quality that causes us to take notice and allow them to become the subject of our contemplation. The questions we ask ourselves may be tender, like the ones I asked after Michael died, or they may shatter our ordinary reality in a way that makes it impossible for us to repair what we had known of our lives before. In this way they function like Franz Kafka's declaration when speaking of his chosen craft: *"Literature,"* he wrote, *"should serve as an ax for the frozen sea within us."*

Isn't this shattering of the frozen sea what Jesus may have felt when he cried into the vacant night, *"My God. My God. Why have You forsaken me?"* I think it is. Very few inquiries in the considerable breadth of the Christian tradition can match the power of this cry to know *Who's there?* But let us look at this closely. Might it not be that because this question—not its answer—was torn from the threshold of what Jesus withstood, it proved a transformative catalyst of his realization as he lay upon the crossroads of life and death?

We don't need to be able to provide an answer. We only need to ask this question and then listen as our intuition begins to stir. This quiet listening is the key to what we might understand once a question appears. This is true whether we are listening to questions others have proposed or to questions of our own. It is listening of a subtle kind. As you practice it you may find that quite often your experience of listening mirrors what lies beneath the question itself. Listening, it may be said, is the field in which question and answer join hands.

Why have You forsaken me? What is Allah or Buddha or God? Is the Lord of Day the same as the God of Night? Did the Mother of All Things also give birth to Evil? Was the blue sky really hatched from an azure stone? What was your face before your parents were born? Each of these questions, and all of the others we ask ourselves, are just our own human spirit seeking to help us return to the wholeness we feel we have lost. They are an attempt to repair our personal world and the world at large. The great Chilean poet Pablo Neruda was a master of such questions, and it is to his *Book of Questions* that I'd like us to turn.

The questions Neruda asks come at an unexpected angle. They enter us viscerally and move about the imagination like the best of poems. It is the very angle of their surprise entry that catches us off guard and immediately appeals to our deepest selves. These questions are not something the rational mind can prepare to receive. Rather, they are more like postcards dashed off to our longing, our need to know who we are. They speak intimately. They whisper in shorthand. Their sense of play and delight causes us to stop for a moment as we consider what we've heard. This is true even when their content is of a most serious kind, which is why we like them. Each question has its own particular nature, and as we allow ourselves to embrace them with our intuition, we begin to discover something of our own nature as well.

Doesn't asking yourself, *"Isn't it true that autumn seems to wait / for something to happen?"* bring the depth of autumn right into your body and mind? Don't you find yourself already there, waiting as if you were autumn itself? How old are you in this picture your imagination provides? Five? Fifty-five? What time of day is it in your mind? What color is the sky? A true question can transform us before we know what has happened.

When the poet asks, *"Why do I go rolling without wheels / flying without wings or feathers?"* or *"Where can you find a bell / that will ring in your dreams?"* he calls to some of the true interests of our deepest self. These questions are like the amulets Robert Creeley brought to mind in the poetic fragment that opened this chapter. Each one possesses a cameo, a treasure, a seed of truth that helps keep love alive. Small as these are, they contain heart questions the poet needed to ask. They reveal some of his longings and dreams.

Neruda was no different from each of us. Doesn't he also speak for you when he asks, *"Is there anything sillier in life / than to be called Pablo Neruda?"* Put your own name there and listen to the sound of your smile of recognition.

Please engage yourself with the practice of questioning in this way. It doesn't matter if you set aside a time to allow for such questioning or if you just begin by taking the time to notice and catch whatever questions you can. (But write these down!) What is important is that when you ask yourself such questions, you don't try to be great at it, or good, or even competent. As you become used to catching questions on the fly, you will notice they have their own weightlessness and light.

When writing your questions down, it is so much more

enjoyable to simply surrender to what they are. Just allow yourself to open the amulet and discover the surprise. Then, when the intuitive connections inside your questions begin to reveal themselves and excite your imagination, follow wherever they may lead. It's a bit like following a butterfly. When it wobbles, you wobble. When it lands, you land. Just follow without judgment. A welcoming curiosity is all you need and your writing will take care of itself.

In his book Neruda asked questions about rice, trains, beer, and snow. He wanted to know how the abandoned bicycle won its freedom and if the world holds anything sadder than a train standing in the rain. He looked at dreams and asked if the father who lives in a dream dies again when the dreamer awakens. *"How old is November?"* he asked, and then he became curious about whether the rose was standing naked or just wearing its only dress. Because he allowed himself to listen, to follow wherever his intuition led as it made the world before him new, each of his questions, rooted in the lives of ordinary things, was authentic and true.

Many things conspired
to tell me the whole story.
Not only did they touch me,
or my hand touched them:
they were
so close
that they were a part
of my own being,
they were so alive with me

that they lived half my life
and will die half my death.

Can you feel his care and wonder? Give yourself a short period in which to sit in your room, look at the objects there with the idea that each one contains a question you had not considered before, and then write each of the questions down. It may help if you decide you will only ask playful questions at first. Let your imagination pose questions that seem to make no sense. Is my computer really a Tasmanian dancer? When she hears the telephone, will the new bride place the rings on her finger?

It can be difficult to be *just* silly, our imagination really does seek ways to help us understand who we are by providing symbolic content. This was shown to me in a poignant way recently when I was playing "the question game" with Tai, my five-year-old son. In the game, I ask one question after another, and Tai's part is to answer each question and give his reason for his answer. As the game developed on this particular day, I realized his replies were showing me a map of his inner life.

"Would you rather be the tallest tree in the world or a cloud?" I asked.

"I'd rather be a cloud."

"And why would you rather be a cloud? A tall tree is a pretty remarkable thing."

"If I was a cloud," he said, "I'd be closer to God."

"Oh," I answered. "That's pretty good. But do you think that a cloud is closer to God than a tree?"

"No," Tai said. "But if I was a cloud and someone needed rain I could rain for them and then I'd be lighter and float up higher in the sky, and then I'd be closer to God."

And we both laughed, but I was moved at how truly his imagination was holding its course.

If you begin with a lighthearted spirit, which was the spirit of the game I played with my son, you may be surprised to discover how easily questions will come. You will also be surprised to discover how significant your playful questions turn out to be. After writing a few of these, allow a slightly more serious tone to enter your questions. *What time is springtime?* can be a serious question, and yet it depends upon the simplicity of a pun.

This exercise works best if you write in one sitting and allow four or five questions to appear one after another. Often, they will spark each other, as did the ones in the question game I played with my son, and before long a whole symbolic language will begin to make itself known. If you do this for only ten minutes several times a week you will have more than enough seed material for you to write longer pieces with authenticity and depth.

Some people have taken this exercise to work with them and began asking questions in the middle of their business day. They let their minds become curious in the way I have suggested, and before long they were seeing the world of order and predictability with new eyes. Simple as it is, this exercise does have the ability to awaken our imaginations and reshape how we experience the world. Whether you ask your questions at home or at the office, please remember to maintain the spirit of open inquiry, always allowing your intuition to lead. Be whimsical. Be serious. Be sensitive to a sudden shift of mood as your images take you somewhere new. Our unconscious mind is always ready to engage us with true content. It is always ready to dance. If we make ourselves available, the kinds of images that come to us in dreams come easily to our waking mind. When we invite them in, every moment of our lives can reveal unasked questions, unheard words. All we have to do is be willing to listen, and to see.

WHEN THE STONE
WOMAN DANCES,
THE MUTE BIRD SINGS

☾

I have a friend, a poet, and sometimes we "talk poetry." Like many other people, she is someone who feels a special connection to stones; and when she holds certain stones in her hand, she does so with what she describes as a feeling of reverence. One day we were talking about this part of her creative and spiritual life, for she often includes stones in her poetry, and she said that the experience of reverence comes quite naturally to her because she feels as if the stones she holds are grandmothers or grandfathers or, sometimes, children.

"They are stone people, very ancient," she said, "even the ones I come to realize are children after I've been with them awhile." I can tell you that she means every word of this, and I can also tell you, from walking with her many times over the years, that she searches for stones wherever she goes in case one might be calling to her.

"How do they call to you?" I once asked. We were on one of our walks.

"They call to me with their silence. The silence of a stone is its voice."

"And how do you hear them, if they speak with silence?"

"I hear them with my whole body. My whole body and mind. Usually I begin to hear a stone calling with the first glance of my eye [as you can see, "talking poetry" is a wonderful language, especially when our senses are set free from their usual limitations and we can hear with our eyes or see with the sensitive touch of our hands] but then, very quickly, as my glance turns to seeing alone and the stone's color and shape fill my eye, its voice moves through my entire body like the sound of an organ filling a cathedral, except the music the stone plays is its silence. It's very erotic, really. Very sexy. When this happens I feel a kind of warmth, or the promise of that warmth, all through me, and I pick up the stone and hold it because my hand understands the silence of a stone in a way that sometimes makes me cry. It's in their weight and the way their shape fits my palm. That's how stones really speak to us, you know." And she gave me a conspiratorial smile.

I think many of us know what my friend is saying, even if we don't talk poetry on a regular basis. Maybe we don't know it about stones precisely, but there is an intuitive eroticism, or relationship, of a very silent and sacred kind between human beings and the things of the natural world. In my friend's case, when the stone's life has spoken sufficiently for her to understand its desire (in order to hear it with greater intimacy she often encloses the stone within her hand and shuts her eyes), she either replaces the stone where she first spotted it—"because it wants to stay with its family," she says—or she holds it awhile longer, listening, before placing it in her pocket and taking it home to join its brother and sister stones on her stone shrine. I've seen this shrine, and it is reverently and beautifully made.

There is a phrase in Indonesian culture for objects that people believe possess an individual essence or soul: *rasa hidup*. *Rasa* means "feeling of" and *hidup* (which I've been told rhymes with *bebop*) means "life." The feeling of life. I think, like my friend, many people share this intuition about supposedly insentient objects. Children seem to naturally see the world with this orientation, and I can clearly remember knowing the essential truth of *rasa hidup* about many objects in my own childhood, a conviction I have never really abandoned. Of course, some will say it is simply a child's projection of his or her human feelings upon the nonhuman world, or a poet's imagination, but there are many people, and indeed whole cultures, who would disagree.

The word *Veda* means "knowledge," and the Vedas are the most sacred scriptures of the Hindu religion, dating back more than thirty-five hundred years, though their precise origin is difficult to date because they were transmitted orally for about a thousand years before they were written down. In the Vedas it is told that the Sanskrit language came into being when the essence of each thing first made its sound known to human beings. When people heard these primordial soundings they realized they were witnessing the self-naming of the physical world, and so the sound each thing made became the word by which it was known.

Imagine for a moment that you live during this time and that one morning, as you walk thoughtlessly through the ancient Indian forest adjacent to your home (I find it a joy to read *thoughtlessly* as an expression of a mind freed from the tethers of our usual thinking), a tree suddenly and for the very first time speaks to you in a language you have never heard before, yet intuitively understand. "Tree," it says, by which it means, "I am This." Imagine that you understand the significance of the tree sounding its name. Then imagine that as you turn in amazement from Tree, and look at what is right beside you, this new object also speaks from the depth of its essential being and says, "Stone." And that Earth makes the sound of its name and then Air and River and Green and Bird and Thunder and Fire and Worm, on and on and on like the eruption of ten thousand seeds until the sound of each and every particle of your world names itself into your mind: "I am This."

It is quite a vision to imagine that we are in the forest of primordial naming. It is as if the entire world has decided to talk poetry at once so that we may learn, through their soundings, the meaning of their lives. Then, when we speak or write their names, they will become real to us, and to those who are touched by our words. They will become known.

∾

Many years ago I translated a poem by the great twentieth-century Spanish poet Juan Ramón Jiménez. I'd like to offer this poem to you now.

Mind, Give Me

Mind, give me
the exact name of things!
. . . that my word may be
the thing itself,
re-created by my soul.
So that all who do not know them
go through me
> *to things;*
all who have forgotten
go through me
> *to things;*
all those who love them
go through me
> *to things . . .*
Mind, give me
the exact name, and yours
and theirs and mine, of things!

I love this poem for its simplicity and depth. It articulates what I believe to be one of the deepest yearnings of human life: that we may make the world new again, and real, and that we may be guided in this by what poet Allen Ginsberg called the *"supernatural extra brilliant intelligent kindness of the soul."* This poem is really a prayer born of the generous vision and need of a poet who knew that once this transformation occurs, *the thing itself* (the things of the world brought beautifully alive) would not be held simply for our own uses, but would benefit others in many ways. Jiménez had confidence in us; he understood that each of us is born with the capacity to know and to speak the exact name to bring this transformation about. He knew that when we do, our unique articulation would also answer our own deepest yearning to know, to remember, and to love.

In order to satisfy this yearning by allowing our words to remain rooted and alive in what is real, some work must be done. The primary focus of this work is to release the grip of our various defenses and free ourselves from as many forms of internal limitation and control as we can. It may sound like a terrible battle is in store. In fact, at this very moment the fearful part of our ego would love to convince us that this is true. Then we might walk away before even making a start. But the nature of the engagement is quite different from what the ego fears. It is not terrible; it is creative and fun. When you take it up, your ability to give yourself completely to what lies before you will be unhindered. Your writing will be shaped by your ability to hear even the most remote regions of both the imagination and the invisible life of things.

This has the effect of igniting what you write. Ezra Pound said that "literature is language charged with meaning." Writing that comes to us from within the things themselves is so connected to life's source that it possesses that charge. The effect is undeniable. Those who read what you have written will feel refreshed as they hear *through the lan-*

guage of your story or poem the waters of a hidden stream flowing by, or the voice of pines and cedars when no wind stirs. Literature that lasts is filled with such presence. It is a walking meditation all its own, except this time readers walk into the imagination of a stranger and find themselves already there.

I call the techniques that help you listen at the root of things while freeing your senses and imagination *soft focus*. These techniques know how to slip beneath your ego's defenses and make it possible for you to approach the exact name of the thing itself as the stone woman dances and the mute bird fills the air with song—which is my way of saying spirit expresses itself everywhere when we set ourselves free.

Usually, when we decide to look at something, we do so with what I think of as "bright eyes." We look really hard, and while this may have its uses—for example, when we want to describe the external details of an object with exact photographic reproduction—most often this approach allows the essence of things to remain out of our line of vision, unseen and therefore unknown. Hard looking ignores the essential, subtle body; what Buddhists call the "suchness" of the thing before us. It works against presence. I find that if we really want to see, we have to close our eyes to our usual way of seeing, click down the brightness of the light, and begin to listen in the shadows.

Paradoxically, soft focus begins with our taking a bright, hard look and noticing each and every component of what is before our eyes, before letting it go. For example, if you are holding a stone, as I am now, really look at it. Notice its shape and size; take a good look at the subtle shading of its color and feel its actual weight as it rests in your palm. After you have enjoyed this vivid encounter with the stone (or whatever you have chosen) for no longer than a minute, move on to the next part of soft focus. This is where you disengage from focusing on the object in the hard and bright way. To do this just cast your gaze downward and turn your head slightly to the side as if you were listening in a thoughtful manner. When you first do this the actual details of the object will recede into your mind and awaken your intuition. This allows you to sense and feel the object in a way that calls forth your personal associations, memories, and metaphorical imagery. It also allows you to know the object in a way that is entirely new. Now close your eyes completely and let your hands roam over what you hold. Rub it on your cheek. Hold it close to your breast. Invent means to approach the object at a more subtle, oblique angle. The emotion and imagery that arise from this experience of intuitive sensing will ignite the content of what you write.

For example, as I look at the stone, it is one thing to use the bright technique to report that "the stone is hard, oblong, weighs about one pound, and has a red line bisecting it from the bottom to the top." It is quite another to approach the stone obliquely and express my experience of this very same stone in a poetic fragment on the order of:

> *Rooted in earth*
> *and sky*
> *a blood line*
> *flows through*

the hardened world.
My father plowed
such fields,
and they broke him
open
as a fractured stone,
until his blood
flowed
into me,
waiting
before the birth
of the world's
first hardness.
Peter, he called
me, without knowing
he had given
me the lineage
and the name
of stone.

Both packets of words rose out of my encounter with the stone, but, as you can see, the example of soft focus awakened personal associations and metaphorical imagery that hopefully expresses something of the stone's life, as well as my own. To bring this about I "lowered my gaze." I placed one ear, as it were, on the stone and one softly focused eye in my own heart and imagination so I could intimately engage the intuitive stirrings provoked by the stone. This lowered gaze made it possible for me to sense the life of the stone while simultaneously feeling the shape and size and color of my own invisible world. The depth of emotion and imagination I found was awakened by this process, and, in the end, I was able to see the stone and myself in a way I had never seen before. This kind of experiential awakening is crucial to writing. It is the key to experiencing ourselves and the things of our world in the spirit of what Zen painter and writer Paul Reps called the *aliving* word.

When you focus softly, intimately working with an object of your choosing, you will discover that your writing is alive with personal realizations, and you will simultaneously experience some essence of the very thing you hold. As I have already mentioned, no matter how vast the universe may appear, there is only one life being lived here, and we live it with all things, individually and together. Soft focus allows us to experience what lies beneath the surface of our physical world with eyes that make that world transparent. When this takes place, the exact name may be known.

One of the elements of soft focus that makes this knowing possible is what I like to think of as *mutual permeation.* I experienced this as the molecules of my own life and the molecules of the stone flowing back and forth, as if the solidity of our bodies and minds had dissolved and we were breathing one breath together. In order to do this, I had to accept that my imagination of this occurrence was real. This caused my usual way of seeing to become disordered so that I no longer had a purely linear, rational experience of the stone or myself. As a result, this unlikely experience further stirred up my intuition and brought forth quite a bit of feeling. The intimate knowing of myself and the stone that resulted was entirely dependent on this shift.

In order to practice this, and to expand its uses in your writing life, I'm going to ask that you make your own hand the object you work with during this next part of soft focus. In the future you may choose an object from the natural world or one that is manufactured. It doesn't really matter. What matters in all of your writing is the quality of attention, of presence, that you bring to yourself and the world.

Please begin by looking at your hand in the usual way. Just notice its shape and size, its subtle coloration, the lines that crisscross or extend across its length and width. Look at the top of your hand: notice the traces of any veins that branch through it; observe the folds and rings in the skin that covers your knuckles. Take a look at the shape of your nails. Then turn your hand over and look at your fingers and palm from the other side. Notice the smoothness or roughness of your skin, then examine the tips of your fingers and the place where your palm meets your wrist. As you observe the top and bottom of your hand in this way, breathe quietly and become aware that you are looking with your eyes. The best way to do this is to consciously choose to place your mind behind your eyes and look through them. This conscious placement of the mind is very important for what comes next.

After you have looked at your hand through your eyes for a minute or so, send your mind lower and look at your hand with your throat. I mean this exactly as I said it. Your throat can apprehend the world in a way quite different from seeing with your eyes, and if you breathe quietly and observantly as you do this, you will experience what I mean.

In "The Narrow Place," I introduced the idea that our bodies are repositories of deep self-knowledge. I want to develop that thought a bit more now to encourage you to use your body as a creative resource for your work. Each part of your body has an entirely unique way of knowing the world, because each has had different experiences particular to its form and function—as eyes, for example, or the throat. Each has strengths and vulnerabilities no other part shares. Each has different memories and associations, even of the same events, and when we choose to perceive from discrete parts of ourselves, these differences come significantly into play.

This method of disordering our usual means of perception by "looking" from different parts of our bodies is soft focus, too. Notice as you look at your hand with your throat how your experience of seeing has changed, how new sensations and emotions have emerged as a result of this kind of sight. Notice what happens in your body. If some memories and surprising associations begin to appear in your psyche and imagination, please continue to breathe quietly and consistently and notice what they are. Our throats are very delicate and significant parts of our bodies and minds; when we apprehend the world from here, it can be quite powerful.

After you have seen with your throat for a minute or two, please continue to hold your hand before you but lower it to the heart area of your solar plexus. Now allow your mind to see through your heart. Maintain a quiet and consistent breath as you do this. This seeing is quite different from both the eyes and the throat. As you did before, notice every sensation, personal association, and image that seeing from the heart brings forth. Notice which things change and which remain the same. Observe what happens to your breathing, to your entire psyche, as your hand moves from throat to heart. Be careful to avoid judgments of any kind at this stage. Only act; only see.

When you have fully seen and experienced your hand from your solar plexus, lower your gaze down to the belly. Allow your breath to deepen as you do this and feel your belly gently rise and fall in a natural way. This tends to increase the feeling of intimacy between your breathing and your hand. As your mind has gradually perceived your hand from eyes through throat and heart to belly, you have also shifted from linear and rational perception to intuitive and emotional knowing. You may or may not have words for what you are experiencing as you look at your hand now, but you will certainly have some feelings involved. Both vague and particular memories also tend to arise as we become comfortable with using this technique.

To heighten your awareness of the differentiated-feeling quality of your experience, please continue to observe your hand while *slowly* raising the focus and placement of your mind from your belly past your heart until you reach your throat again. This is a very powerful channel through the center of our bodies. As you do this, notice any subtle shifts or changes of feeling or perception that occur. Then, working slowly and with great care, bring the attention of your mind back to your eyes. Observe any changes as you do this. After resting here a moment, bring your focus slowly back down to the area of your solar plexus and continue to look at your hand. Do you notice how the quality of feeling changes again, how your way of knowing and the content and nature of what you know shifts as you locate the vessel of perception in different parts of your body? Explore this for as long as you like before moving on, but remember to always shift your attention with care.

Please allow the focus and attention of your mind to rest in your belly again. Settle in there and breathe with a natural calm. After you have done this for some time, continue to look at your hand while lowering it down the channel that runs through the center of your body to the area of your genitals. For reasons that may be fairly obvious, certain mystical traditions consider the area of the genitals the root. This part of our bodies holds so many memories, so much visceral knowing about who and what we are, and what we have experienced in our lives, that it is a primary storehouse of our creativity. While it is true that eros may be found in every part of ourselves, our genitals are its natural home.

Look at your hand with your genital area now, breathing slowly and deeply as you do. The magnetic attraction between our genitals and physical contact is so primary that you eventually may want to explore "looking" by touching. I ask you not to do this for now. There is a powerful difference in how we perceive and intuit when we come into actual physical contact with something and when we do not. At this time, you will gain the most from this experience if you touch without touching, so please keep a distance between the vessel of perception and the object perceived.

Many times, if I am not sure what I am feeling as I talk with someone, or if I am writing and can't quite grasp the nature of what I need to say, I lower my gaze, place my attention at one of these points in my body, and perceive from there. When I do, my intuition speaks to me in a language I have learned to trust and understand. It is not the rational, cognitive language insisted upon in our ordinary lives, but because it is rooted in intuition and sensation, in *rasa hidup*, the "feeling of life," it is a language we all know. For some it may be a bit like talking poetry without words.

Time to write. Please move your attention slowly upward through your body from the root and see with your eyes. Maintain the quiet composure of your body and mind, take out some writing materials, and begin to write. The compelling experiences that soft focus brings to life tend to help your writing take care of itself. It is for this reason that I will refrain from offering a specific, prescriptive exercise here. In your own experience of your body, you already know what needs to be said. Trust this. If you like, feel free to repeat any part of the process while you write to reignite your experience or your words. At will, you can join the stone woman as she dances or hear the mute bird's song.

If you make a regular practice of using these techniques, you will discover how deeply they nourish your creative and spiritual life. They will become as natural to your way of knowing as breathing. And breathing, as we know, is what keeps us and the word alive.

DIVINE BREATH

((

I have asked you to maintain an awareness of your breathing as you begin each exercise and move from one stage to the next. Following and working with the breath is a basic meditative technique found in contemplative traditions throughout the world. This is because when we breathe consciously, our breath creates a bridge that unifies our body and mind. As you have become more familiar with this technique, you may have noticed that a soft, almost transparent light seems to pervade your being as your breath becomes more stable and your body / mind begins to calm. Some people say they feel more transparent, and yet paradoxically more solid and real, when they establish this unifying bridge. Whatever your personal experience, the important thing to know is that the pervasive clarity you experience as a result of conscious breathing instills your work with the spirit and energy of life itself. It is an originating and sustaining source.

In the beginning of the Torah, which according to Jewish belief is the Law given to the Jewish people in a divinely created alphabet, the phrase *a wind from God* appears. This phrase has also been translated as *the spirit of God* and *the breath of the Divine.* The Hebrew word which gives rise to these phrases is *ruach.* We are told that at the very dawn of Creation, *"when darkness was upon the face of the deep"*—a phrase I dearly love when applied to our own imaginations and creative process before we write—this spiritual wind, this *holy soul of the Creator,* swept through all parts of the primordial darkness and *"hovered over the face of the waters."*

I'd like to suggest that you begin to integrate the teaching that will follow from this image by becoming aware of how naturally and easily the air flows in and out of your nostrils. Notice how effortlessly your belly rises and returns with each breath. We don't have to think our breathing into existence; it's just a part of who and what we are. For most people, the existence of this breath defines being alive. After all, when a baby is first born and, at the other end of life, when someone appears to have died, we look to see if they are breathing. Please maintain a light awareness of your breath and, after reading the following paragraph, which contains a few questions, put the book down, close your eyes, and listen to the sound that your own breath makes in its natural flow.

Here are my questions: Where is *ruach,* this Divine wind or spirit or breath that swept through the Great Dark even before the Creation? Has it disappeared? Was it only something that may have happened once, a long time ago? As you allow these questions to settle in and take root in your imagination, please consider the following. The Jewish tradition teaches that God, the Divine Plenty, is all-pervasive and eternal. This implies that a holy essence can still be found in each thing of our world. Now stop reading for a few moments and begin to listen to the sound of your breath. Don't try to come up with an answer to whether *ruach* remains or has disappeared. Even when our intellect satisfies itself, it does not know things completely as they really are. For now, just close your eyes and allow your breathing to be the sound of both the question and the answer in your ears.

When you pick up this book again, please read more slowly than you usually do. This will help you to stay in touch with your breath, a practice that clarifies and, one might say, oxygenates the imagination. As I've already mentioned, we are told that the Divine forms a human being out of the dust of the earth and then releases the breath of life, called *neshamah* in Hebrew, into the nostrils of this human creation, who would become known as Adam. In the tradition it is said that this breath, born of *ruach,* forms the intimate, primordial bond joining humans to the Creator because it flows directly between them. Many teachings also consider *neshamah* the personal soul. I find it literally and metaphorically significant that the same word is used for *breath* and what we usually call *soul.* In terms of creative work, it is essential to note that only after Adam received *neshamah* did he awaken and come to life.

Please continue your calm and conscious breathing now, aware that your own breath is not only the bridge that unifies your body and mind, but that it also is considered the primary connection between you and what is called the Divine. As you let these teachings in, allow any thoughts and feelings they generate to circulate freely within you, but don't try to grasp them in any intellectually specific way or even attempt to remember a single one. You don't have to. Your awakened intuition is already doing what it was made to do, and the spacious nature of your imagination will remember everything you need in order to express yourself with authenticity and true feeling when it is time to write.

The teachings you've just read contain a very few of the basic elements of Jewish cosmology: Human breath is rooted in Divine breath, and Divine breath is inherent in human breath, reflecting the interdependent nature of the human and the Divine. This idea of human and Divine interdependence may be new to many of you, but it is so inherent in Jewish tradition that one rabbi told me it is believed that when human beings withdraw from God, both the people who withdraw and God are diminished. It is a revolutionary idea. It forces us to look at the fabric of reality in a whole new way. Of course, from a physical or purely psychological standpoint it makes sense: Any part of ourselves that is not nourished weakens. It is why consistent practice is such a crucial part of our spiritual and creative lives. But do human beings really have such influence in relation to the Creative Principle, which is another name for God?

Please focus on your breathing now with a light and spacious concentration. There is no need for you to think anything in particular as you attend to this. After following your breath for a few complete cycles of inhalation and exhalation, allow breath that is both human and Divine to move through you as you *in*spire—taking in all the nourishment that sustains your life—and *ex*pire, breathing out what is known in meditative traditions as "the dying breath."

To begin the following exercise, please stand in a comfortable position, breathe naturally, without any special effort at all, and let your body relax. After a few moments of this, your body and mind should become increasingly undefended and open. Now just allow yourself to receive what I'm going to say without rushing to think or answer or know anything at all. One good way to work with a question you hear is to allow it to enter your body gently, the way a breeze enters a forest and begins to play among the trees. The trees don't have to do anything but stand there while the breeze moves through and around them, touching first the bark or leaves on one side, then the soft moss on the other, until it has encircled the entire tree.

You have already considered whether the original wind of creation continues to exist. Please ask yourself how long the breath of life that moves through you so freely at this very moment has been here. How long have these literal molecules circulated in one form or another in our world? Approach this question as you did the one before. Continue to breathe naturally and allow the question to touch your imagination lightly. There is no need to think of any particular answer. Since the experiential part of this exercise is a crucial element of awakening to our deeper selves before we write, just allow this question to sufficiently become part of what you are.

The great haiku poet Matsuo Bashō said that when we see or hear things from within the things themselves, we are able to record them in our hearts. This goes for all of the questions and teachings in this book. When you allow them to be heard from within themselves, you will come to understand them in a new way.

After you have considered how long your breath has been part of the world, extend your inquiry to include the molecules that make up your entire body. How long have these been around? How long has all of your body circulated around and around in our world, transforming from one form to another? Please engage this with your whole body and mind, allowing yourself to feel the question as it moves through every part of you. It is a habit to feel we must come up with an answer to every question. Please practice hearing this question once again simply as an experience of yourself, as if it arose from the depths of your own mind. The ability to listen deeply without a single thought is a powerful tool of writers and mystics alike. It awakens all the personal associations our intuition holds and brings these to our conscious minds.

Once you have allowed yourself to fully embody these questions, you may begin the next part of the exercise. Take a look at the four lines on page 98 and repeat each line of this Divine Breath meditation to yourself. While repeating these words, allow yourself at least two minutes to experience what each line suggests, though of course you may explore each for as long as you like. A good way to do this is to close your eyes and silently say the line to yourself several times as you enter the imagination it describes. Allow the imagination to fill you with each repetition. When you feel ready, move on to the next line and repeat the process until you have worked with all four lines.

Divine Breath

Breathe in the Divine, breathe out the human.
Breathe in the human, breathe out the Divine.
Breathe in the Divine, breathe out the Divine.
Breathe in the human, breathe out the human.

When you have worked with all the lines and completed the exercise to your satisfaction—there is no "right" amount of time prescribed, though I suggest you do take your time— breathe normally, naturally, and feel your feet right beneath you on the floor. Techniques that utilize the breath have extraordinary benefits, but they also require that we feel our selves solidly here when we are through.

Now it is time to write. Please maintain contact with your experience and begin writing freestyle for twenty to thirty minutes, allowing yourself to follow any of the feelings, associations, thoughts, sensations, or impressions this meditation has brought you. If you like, you may go back and repeat parts of the exercises you found particularly provocative, useful, or moving. Remember, when the spirit or wind of creativity is brought to our tasks, and when we follow the example of the Creator and breathe life into what we undertake, life itself awakens and is new.

NAKED MIND

☾

In the spirit of invention that partly defined the early years of the twentieth century, poet Ezra Pound urged writers to take their theme and subject and *make it new.* This was part of his effort to help American writing break free from the formal strictures and imagination of the European past. He felt that when writing is conceived of and created with the breath of new life, meaning will burst alive upon the page. Every writer who has embraced this challenge by shedding the ideas, metaphors, and imagination of the past while seeking new means of personal expression has discovered it is true. Writing in this way encourages us to see with new eyes, touch with new hands. It helps us to engage the world with a nakedness of heart and mind that allows us to know things from within themselves so we may render them real in our writing.

Naked mind is a phrase I use to express this complete openness of disposition. It is a sensibility that is spacious and clear; one that takes in the world without prejudging a single thing. Whereas in the West we tend to separate heart and mind, the Chinese character pronounced *shin* simultaneously expresses both and thereby emphasizes the unity of their essential relationship: heart and mind as one. It is in this sense that I use the word *mind.* It is the mind most needed when we write. It receives what appears before us with a freshness that makes it possible for the world to be appreciated in its own terms. Each stone, each leaf, each blue sky comes alive for us when experienced with naked mind.

Despite all the weight of history, and all the countless other human beings who have lived, the world is new for each of us. We experience our lives as if we were the first person on Earth. Belonging solely to us are the first warm touch, the first pain, the first love, and the first love lost. No matter how vividly we may carry others' descriptions in our minds, no one else's experience supersedes our own. But after a while we tend to lose the edge of original experience and unconsciously rely on thoughts and feelings engendered by our previous encounters. We distance ourselves from the experience at hand. In Zen, this conceptualizing about life instead of really living is sometimes called "putting a head on your head." But you don't need to put a head on your head; especially a head that is facing the past.

In order to avoid this tendency, it is crucial for writers to cultivate naked mind. This promotes and protects our ability to experience life directly, to feel the full reach and heart of the world pounding in our chest. Suddenly the grass, the reflected evening light on city buildings, even our loved ones, come alive within us as if we have never seen them before, truly known for the very first time. What a gift.

While the immediacy and power of such experiences may seem frightening to some, more often than not the experience confirms our connection with all things. The openness and intimacy that occurs when we engage life with naked mind allows us to experience ourselves and our world in a way that is warm, full, and embracing. One student who had been working with naked mind for some time told me he felt he could substitute the word *intimacy* for the phrase *naked mind* because it is such a pervasive part of the experience. Because of this intimacy, we can say that naked mind is the red of the leaf as autumn comes on and it is our seeing of that leaf on the tree. It is the smooth gray flank of a boulder we lean against and it is the sudden flash of a red-tailed hawk over the deep-green ridge of pines. It is wind, transparent in the highest branches; the freshly dipped wing of a calligrapher's brush flying across the page; the green of lettuce in your garden; the roar of galaxies and grasses, snowfalls and rains as they flow in your arteries and veins. It is not just an experience of ourselves *in* the world. It is our self, our Big Self, *as* the world entire, found in all its miraculous detail and design.

A few people over the years have asked if naked mind can be considered the intuitive pathway that connects us to all of life. This is part of it, of course, but it is not all. Since its nature is to be full each instant of the whole, it is what our intuition depends upon. It might be thought of as an outdoor amphitheater in which we experience things exactly as they are. When haiku master Bashō wrote his famous enlighten-ment poem

> *Old pond*
> *frog jumps in—*
> *the sound of water*

the sound he heard awakened him and filled the universe because of naked mind.

"But how do we get there?" a young man asked after I introduced naked mind to a workshop. I could see he was rearing to go, if only I would tell him where.

"There is no *going* to naked mind," I told him. "Of course, there are ways you can nourish its emergence in your life, and this workshop will give you the tools, but naked mind is not some place or thing you are lacking and have to attain. It is something you already are. Little by little, as you cease to cherish your opinions and practice some of the other techniques that shed the layers covering your true self, naked mind will be revealed. You will be revealed to yourself *as* naked mind, which you have been from the start. Don't you feel relieved?"

"Not really," he said a bit nervously. "But I'm willing to try."

Everyone in the workshop laughed, but I told him, "That 'not really' you just said is so raw, so completely undefended, I think you are an advanced practitioner of naked mind!"

~

A number of years ago, at Harvard University, a meeting between two extraordinary Buddhist masters was announced. One was Korean Zen master Dae Soen Sa Nim, known for holding an object in his hand and striking the floor with his Zen master's stick while demanding, "What is it?! What is it?!" of students who were startled out of their skins. This was his dramatic but compassionate attempt to help them penetrate the nature of reality. I had the opportunity to study with this wonderful master a number of times, and I can attest to his wisdom, humor, and great compassion. The other was the venerable Tibetan Buddhist teacher Kalu Rinpoche, known for his refined, almost transparent, yet dynamic teachings of the Buddhist Way.

The encounter had been billed as a sort of Buddhist wrestling match between two enlightened masters, and so the auditorium was filled with a highly energized audience of students and faculty when these two extraordinary teachers entered from opposite sides of the hall and took the stage. Dae Soen Sa Nim appeared without a translator, but Kalu Rinpoche's use of English was not as strong, and so he was accompanied by a trusted friend.

After the audience calmed down, the masters sat quietly for a few moments. Then, without warning, Dae Soen Sa Nim produced an object from within his robes, held it before Kalu Rinpoche's eyes, and demanded in the style for which he was famous, "What is it?! What is it?!" The object he held in his hand was an orange. I know from experience that in this moment his entire being was a smile, but he made this demand with all the seriousness and force he could muster.

Kalu Rinpoche looked at the orange and appeared a bit confused. He leaned over to whisper into the ear of his translator, and then his translator leaned over and whispered back into Kalu's ear. This went on for some time, with each of them earnestly looking at the object in the Korean master's hand and then whispering further serious and heated consultation into the other's ear. All this time, Dae Soen Sa Nim sat unmoving with the object clearly visible and the audience spellbound in their seats.

Finally, after some last-minute consultation, Kalu's translator spoke.

"With all respect, Rinpoche would like to know: Don't you have oranges in Korea?"

With that, the audience howled with good-natured laughter. The two masters stood and bowed to each other, and then left the stage.

In producing the orange, Dae Soen Sa Nim was not simply playing the trickster, though he certainly has the trickster spirit within him. When he asks, "What is it?!" he is inviting an answer that demonstrates the true nature of existence. Of course, Kalu Rinpoche understood this. But he also understood that while he might choose to reply in a way that demonstrated the fact that an orange manifests the interdependent nature of all things, an orange is still an orange. And with a wise humor to match his Korean friend, he played on this fact to the delight of all.

Such demonstrations are part of traditional Zen teaching. Their purpose, like the purpose of many spiritual practices, is to help us to understand the big and small picture of all things just as they are—to see with naked mind. Likewise, it is beneficial for writers and artists to cultivate this ability. The more we do, the more transparent the world appears, and the more this transparency becomes a strength in our creations. In the end, the practice of naked mind can even help us to understand the deepest truth of what we are. An exhortation to cultivate our understanding until it is complete— one that I have always found inspiring—comes from the mystical teachings of Kabbalah. It is not enough to understand the meaning of the black letters on the white parchment of the Torah, we are told. We must also understand the white letters made by the space *between* the black letters if we are truly to understand the Word of God.

I have used naked mind as a way to directly experience the world for as long as I can recall. It makes it possible for me to suspend my personal preferences and take a risk by quieting the inner voices that seek to disturb my concentration. No one can force naked mind to show up at will, but you can cultivate the techniques that invite it to come alive, like focusing softly and developing a slow and steady breath as you work. After working with this for a while you will be amazed at how readily naked mind emerges. Sometimes it does so all on its own.

One morning, as I was sitting quietly in my studio beside the river, which had grown quite full with winter rains, the sound of the water rushing by filled my heart and mind. Of course, at first I was just listening, but after some time I became aware that my experience was no longer just a matter of hearing in the usual way. I had become so immersed in the sound, it was as if I had become the river. This was the intimate functioning of naked mind.

As I sat there and continued to experience the sound of rushing water, I felt within its constant modulation a stillness that, like the feeling of intimacy, is one of the characteristics of naked mind. It was a stillness at the heart of the river. Since we maintain the ability to choose when working with naked mind, I turned my attention to this stillness and let it become pervasive. After some time I heard within the simultaneous roar and stillness of the river another sound. It was the steady sound of my own breath as it filled and drained me of life. I sat there for quite a while and experienced myself as the sound of the river, the stillness within it, and the sound of my own human breathing.

What is it?! What is it?! I wondered after my meditation was completed. A question had caught me and would not let go.

It is the sound of the river. And the sound of my own breathing, I told myself.

Yes. But there is something else involved. Something I can't quite grasp. Something I want to name. What is that?

In order to ask this question in a way that would allow my intuitive capacity to flow, I began to write. In the end, I wrote a poem called "The Beautiful Particulars," which I quote in part on page 107.* The beginning of the poem incor-

---

*The full text of this poem can be found in the appendix.

porates some of the realizations that ultimately came as a result of this experience of naked mind.

Among the beautiful particulars
with a naked mind

I walk in leaf shadow
which covers my head

beneath the sky,
the cool river guiding me

to a cool death so
I may hold in my heat

a temperature the universe
has known, expansive

in its contraction,
as I am

in my own small
way, breathing

what the whole universe has
brought me,

to keep me
alive— . . .

The exercise that follows gives you an opportunity to explore the practice of naked mind. I first heard the teaching it is based upon during a retreat with Chagdud Tulku

Rinpoche in the late 1970s. When he was finished speaking, I felt so connected to all of life and so grateful for this connection that I was moved to tears. According to the Tibetan Buddhist view of existence, at one time or another each atom of the universe has been our mother, and we have nourished each atom into existence as well. Just hearing this teaching changed the way I experienced sitting in the room. I looked at the other people differently. I looked at the light that came through the windows with new eyes. I felt more nurtured by the air I was breathing than ever before. And I wanted to protect that air, that light, those people, in a way that felt intimate and profound.

After the retreat I began to think about giving birth and being born quite differently, and a new thought occurred to me. When we conceive of our origin, we usually think of human conception and birth and say, reasonably enough, that our mothers gave birth to us. That's where our interest ends. But as I considered this miraculous if common truth I began to focus on an element of being born I had never really appreciated before, one that fills me with as much awe as the fact of birth itself: I used to live inside my mother. I lived there, inside her body, for nine months. Of course, we all know this in an intellectual way—it hardly comes as news—but allowing the intellect to be the only part of us that knows something puts a distance between ourselves and our lives. It prevents us from experiencing the miracle life truly is. After all, life isn't just thinking, despite what Descartes had to say; life is direct experience. This is why writing that embodies direct experience is so compelling.

When I lived inside the body of my mother, she was the entire world to me. She was my earth, and she was my sky. She was my rivers. She was the weather. She was the sun. She was my absolute physical world and, of course, even more; she was what may be called the subtle or invisible world. But while I was living inside her body, we could say that my mother was living inside the body of the world. The body of the world was her earth and her sky. Her rivers. Her weather. Her sun. Her subtle or invisible world. And, though I was me, living inside of her, and we were two bodies, somehow only one body was there at the very same time. When I really look at this, I see the same phenomena was true for my mother living in the body of the world. There were also apparently two bodies, but at the same time, somehow, there was only one.

If we follow this a little further we see that the body of what we call the world is living in the larger universe, just like a child inside its mother. And taken together, each of the countless animate and inanimate beings and objects of the universe form just one body. One life. If you've ever been on a retreat where you practiced slow-walking meditation with a group you may have experienced this. There are many individuals walking, but you walk as one body, you breathe as one body, you act as one body. During such times, you experience the fabric of silence as a most treasured companion, and a feeling of great intimacy is present. You not only feel intimate with the people around you, you feel intimate with your physical environment as well, including the wooden floor that supports you or, if you are walking outside, the ground, the plants, the flowers, the trees, and the sky. Everything is included in your step. Because this is true, you are able to experience each moment with great clarity and presence, which, like intimacy and stillness, are primary characteristics of naked mind. It is a kind of knowing.

Think of the deep knowing of one another, the intuitive intimacy that my mother and I shared during those first nine months. It is not the knowing associated with conceptual thinking. It is a knowing that is natural, intimate, immediate, and direct. In essence, it is no different from the way a maple leaf experiences the cooling air and begins to turn red. It is the knowing we experience with naked mind.

I hope the all-encompassing nature of naked mind combines with the Tibetan Buddhist teaching on mothers to make it clear why I say that we *are* this intimate world. After all, the entirety of existence can be found in us, right where we are. Once we take this to heart, everything we encounter becomes an opportunity for us to have some direct experience of ourselves that we may not have previously known. It gives us a chance to express the intimacy of our lives in a way that deepens our connections, nourishes our spirit, and makes life startling and new. As the ninth-century Zen master Tozan wrote in a poem expressing his realization:

> *When you understand self which includes everything*
> *You have your true way.*

In order to begin this exercise, please keep these teachings in mind and go for a walk in your intimate world. Be sure to bring your writing materials along. If some of the images from this chapter accompany you, allow them to wash over you like the waters of a stream, but don't feel you have to hold on to a single one. It is more important to be as present as you can during your walk than to recall any individual idea.

As you begin, please walk slowly, though not so slowly that you call attention to yourself if you are on a crowded street. Gradually synchronize your breathing with your walking until you feel quite unified in body and mind. Then bring to mind the Tibetan Buddhist understanding of what you are moving through and really open your eyes. At first, various thoughts or hungry ghosts may attempt to block your way. If they do, just maintain your commitment to stay open during this walk and to allow yourself to experience an intimate connection with something that appeals deeply to your heart and mind.

If you like, find *mother* in something you may never have considered before. Or, perhaps, you may find yourself *as* mother or father. When you settle on something, please allow the feeling of intimacy I've been discussing to permeate your experience as you engage this part of the world that has brought you into being and that you have brought into being as well. Allow yourself as much time as you need to sit or stand before it and breathe with a quiet and calm concentration as you participate in this experience of naked intimacy.

As one student of mine walked in a city park he began by thinking in a conceptual way that the air he was breathing kept him alive, and so, in essence, it might be considered his mother. Then, as he continued to walk, he began to think that the air on his face felt like a mother's caress. He said his own mother had never touched him in that way and yet, when he let the air be his mother, he realized how deeply he had wanted it. As he thought about these experiences he realized how many elements went into creating the very air that nourished him now. It was quite moving, he said, and a bit overwhelming to realize that even time and space were involved. "It pushed all my boundaries," he told me. "I stopped being certain of where I ended and other things began." Then he imagined that his face really was a kind of mother to the air. He felt the air's sentience and began to think that just possibly the air felt nourished by the pleasure it gave him. This made him laugh out loud and begin to reject his whole experience, but it also awakened a tenderness that filled him with a great and quiet joy. When he sat down to write after his walk, he noticed that a pervasive gentleness, a connection to all things, still seemed to surround him. It made his writing come alive in a way it never had before.

When you feel ready, please go to some peaceful place where you can nourish the experience you've just had and begin to write. Start off by noting the salient feelings or thoughts that arose during your experience. Be sure to write each of these down completely. As you do, follow any of the intuitive connections that arise. From time to time, close your eyes to recall the moments where you felt the greatest intimacy. This will reinvigorate your direct experience and bring a vitality to your writing. When you have completed your writing, please read it over and be sure to welcome each and every experience and perception without judgment. Then take a deep and quiet breath.

One friend, who is also a student I have worked with for a number of years, uses this exercise whenever she feels the need to "reconnect my wires," as she calls it. I like the phrase. She goes to a natural setting outside the city in which she lives and walks along a particular streambed that has some large boulders upon which she likes to sit. It is in this atmosphere that she is most able to follow the teachings in this chapter and practice naked mind.

This woman lost all contact with her father when he and her mother divorced. She was very young. She remembers running after her father as he drove away in a scene that is still hurtful to recall. When she goes to her place in the country, she makes a point of sitting quietly beside the stream, focusing on her breath, and feeling the solidity and strength of the boulder beneath her. "I know it sounds a bit crazy," she said when she told me about her first experience, "but I sat there and used the sound of my breathing to clear my mind, just as you suggested. Then I allowed myself to think of that boulder as my father, and before I knew it, I began to understand in a visceral way that it really *was*. That damned boulder wasn't just a psychological projection," she said, *"it became my father!* Its strength and presence filled me completely, as if it were my birth father in the flesh. And maybe it is. I felt a depth of connection with stone that I have never felt before, though I've been seeking solace in the natural world for fifty years. Who knew that stone could feel so vulnerable, so soft?" Then she began to laugh. "You know, it's a little embarrassing to admit," she said, "and I suppose it was only because the sun was so hot, but I felt the father's warmth as well. And, dammit, this time I knew it was a father who wasn't going away!"

The connections and intuitive intimacy you experience while combining naked mind with the teachings in this chapter can draw the map of your family tree across territories previously uncharted and unknown. It can reconnect your wires in ways that nourish your life, as it did for the young man and my friend. I encourage you to work with these teachings many times and to use all of your discoveries in your writing. This will extend the reach and power of both your understanding and your expression. As you incorporate the practice of naked mind into your daily activities, your bond with all of life increases. It is an extraordinarily inspiring, healing, and pragmatic way to name yourself and your world anew while placing beneath your feet an essential part of your pathway home.

NAMING

☾

Infant Joy

I have no name
I am but two days old.—
What shall I call thee?
I happy am
Joy is my name,—
Sweet joy befall thee!

Pretty joy!
Sweet joy but two days old.
Sweet joy I call thee:
Thou dost smile.
I sing the while
Sweet joy befall thee.

—WILLIAM BLAKE

Writing is the process of naming a particular world into existence. Our ability to find the true names to express that world is directly related to our ability to extend our usual boundaries so that we write beyond the limitations of our personal lives, as I've just described. This helps our writing to be compelling, and true, so that the reality of the world we create cannot be denied.

There are as many ways for us to come into a name, or for a name to come to us, as there are cultural and spiritual traditions. Names are given to honor the dead, protect the living, and express what is believed or hoped to be the spirit or fate of a newborn. I have already touched upon the Judeo-Christian belief that each thing of the universe was brought into existence through the divine articulation of its name. I have also mentioned the Vedic teaching that the soul of each thing spoke its name into the world. It is clear that the importance of naming is anchored in our consciousness by powerful, sacred roots.

In Zen Buddhism some names, called *dharma* names, are given to those who are newly ordained to express what their teachers perceive to be their nature. Other dharma names are given to encourage students to cultivate the qualities the name expresses. I once heard Zen master Dainin Katagiri-roshi say that *Dainin,* the name given to him by his teacher, means "Great Patience." Then he began to turn down the corners of his mouth in a mock frown that became almost a signature for this wonderful man and said, with a coy sparkle in his voice, "Mmm. Great Patience. Great Problem. Great Problem for me."

About two years before my son was born I had a dream. Names like to populate dreams, and many traditions rely on the dreaming of a parent, a grandparent, or a shaman for the gathering of names. The night of this particular dream I was participating in a thirty-day Zen practice period called *Ango*, or "Peaceful Dwelling." In the dream my wife came to me and said, "Tell me something loving." Immediately, I responded, *"Thây!"* (pronounced *tai* as in *tai chi*), by which I meant that if we had a son we should consider naming him after Zen teacher Thich Nhat Hanh, a man I had studied and worked with who had been particularly tender to me at a time when I needed such care. Many people know that Thây, as he is often called, was also a peace activist during the Vietnam war and was nominated by Martin Luther King for the Nobel Peace Prize.

After the thirty days of practice I went home and told my wife the dream. She liked the sound of both the origin of the name and the name itself and agreed it would be a wonderful name for a boy. Of course, there was no baby on the horizon yet, but still . . . Several weeks later my wife told me that in her reading she discovered that one of the meanings of the Chinese ideogram pronounced *tai* was *peaceful.* Perfect. The circle comprised of inner and outer worlds completes itself in a name. And as I write these words, our son Tai is playing in the garden. Peacefully.

My name is Peter. But as I mentioned in discussing the narrow place, my name is also Pesach because this is the name the rabbis gave to me eight days after I was born to celebrate my covenant with God. My mother chose Peter because, for the first time in the history of our family, she did not want to follow the Ashkenazy Jewish tradition of naming a newborn after someone who had died, to memorialize the dead person, but wanted to name a child for no other reason than beauty and for the beautiful feeling it gave her to say the name.

"Peter," she told me, "was that name. I just loved it, that's all. It was right after the war and there had been so much death and sadness, so many people killed in that terrible war. I didn't want you to carry that with you into your life. I wanted something different for you. I wanted you to carry beauty."

The genesis of a name can be as powerful and personal as that. Sometimes names arise from a dream or a story, and sometimes names begin the story not yet told or brought into the real. In both cases, names have a concentrated power to express our outer and inner lives in ways I find quite potent and magical. One tradition of naming that I love comes from the Swampy Cree, an Algonquian Indian people who throughout history have been hunters, trappers, and fishermen in an area ranging from the Canadian subarctic to the savanna of south-central Canada. Part of the Swampy Cree naming tradition is to give a name that has been "earned" because of various childhood episodes, affinities, special talents, and even obsessions. Here is a story about a girl named Larger Ears, told by author Howard Norman, who learned it from Samuel Makidemewabe, a traditional Cree storyteller.

Larger Ears

She had large ears, and this seemed
to please her. Even the time a man joked at her ears
and said they were BATS,

she chose to believe it! She said to him, "Yes,
you are right. They are bats!
I'm glad you came to tell me.
And I will send them into your house
THIS VERY NIGHT to hover
and listen over your face!"

This quickly stopped
his joking.

Also, she liked to listen to *large* sounds
with those large ears.
Maybe the two things
went together.
Before storms, she would sit along the edge
of a lake, EVEN AFTER IT BEGAN RAINING,
and listen to thunder.
Sometimes she shouted back
to it, "Louder, I can hardly hear you!"
Even though the rest of us
had our hands over our ears, as we sat
inside our houses.

Listening with our smaller ears.

I find this so evocative of the spirit of the girl, so honoring of
her unique character as well as her inner strength and beauty.
When I read this poem I have no doubt of the depth of her
connection with her own way of being, perhaps initially
brought about by pain, and of the spiritual rootedness she
feels in the natural world. Notice that the seed of this telling
was simply the personal significance of two small words:
Larger Ears. Yet the telling expressed so much.

Before moving to the writing exercise, I want to give you one more example of naming from the Swampy Cree.

Born Tying Knots

When he came out, into the world,
the umbilical cord
was around his toes.
This didn't trouble us,
that he was tying knots *that* early.
We untied it.

Later, he heard his birth
story.
It caused him to begin tying knots again.
He tied things up near his home,
TIGHT, as if everything might float away
in a river.

This river came from
a dream he had.

House things were tied up
at night. Shirts, other clothes too,
and a kettle. All those things
were tied to his feet
so they wouldn't float away
in the river he dreamed.
You could walk in
and see this.

Maybe the dream stopped
because it was no longer comfortable
to sleep with shirts tied to him.
Or a kettle.

After the dream stopped,
he quit tying things,
EXCEPT for the one night he tied up
a small fire.
Tied up a small-stick fire!
The fire got loose its own way.

What is your name? Having read what is written above, what name can you discover for yourself that expresses a seed of the true person you are? Once again, allow yourself to just listen to the question and notice what words or phrases intuitively rise from the unseen ground of your being. You will enjoy this part of the exercise most if you simply allow names that come to you to be received unhindered by quick judgments that might seek to prevent you from really exploring the truth they carry. Be playful when you do this. Dance with the possibilities. Remember names like Born Tying Knots and Larger Ears. Be serious. We never know what seemingly offhand bit of internal gossip may actually be the very seed of true expression we need. Our usual ego can be very tricky. It can even allow us a thought while preventing us from recognizing its importance or truth. This is why I emphasize allowing the names to come to you, willy-nilly, without encountering a guard at the door. After all, *everything is permitted in the imagination.*

Since this permission is granted by the simple fact that you want and need it now, please write a list of no less than fifteen words or phrases that could name a part of you that wants to become known. Remember to remain open and receptive as you make this list, putting no pressure on yourself to come up with the one right name that says it all. An attitude of joy, an anticipation of discovery and release, will help you to come up with wonderful names. When you are done, scan the list and find a name you not only recognize as true in some way that you may not have understood before (often the true name is the one that tickles you or makes you nervous), but one that seems to have come to you so you can tell its story. As Swampy Cree storyteller Samuel Makidemewabe said, "To say the name is to begin the story."

And so you should. Settle on one name, knowing you can work with others from the list later on, and begin to tell tales about it. Tell where it came from. Show it in action at its best, its worst, its trickiest, its most serious. Use this telling to discover and explore the true meaning this name holds for you. Let your telling show how this name expresses an essence of what you are or contains other wisdom. Allow yourself to dream this name as the true carrier of your spiritual being. In the telling, give yourself the gift of knowing who you are more deeply than you did before the name appeared. It is a gift such names can bring.

Then, just for fun, turn things around. Begin another piece in which you tell a fantastic tale about your name. Make something totally unexpected happen. Expand space. Shrink time. Complicate things for your name by having it fall in love with another of the names on your list—one that it can't stand. Put it under a spell. Spread rumors that make its hair fall out. Then let its wisdom save the day.

In many spiritual traditions it is said that every time a name is spoken the attributes signified by the name are released into the world. Isn't that why children are called Hope or Faith? Wasn't it my mother's desire that the name Peter always signify and bring beauty to the world, and didn't she tell me its origin so that my own name would always point me in that direction? If we look with care, we will see that Born Tying Knots and Larger Ears also release the virtues and attributes their stories hold once these stories are spoken out loud. Please follow this tradition in the writing you do now.

Once you connect to the name that has chosen you (we should not underestimate the ability of these names to choose us, you know), the most important things are for your telling to release the hidden meanings of your chosen name and for you to be joyful as you write. Enjoy the freedom of imagining what your name may be, and may become, as you speak about it in the world.

THE BONES BENEATH
THE BONES

☾

all things rise, transparent
into the forms of the world

it is the emptiness we see
a stone

the hand around it
there is a brightness

but no one knows where it comes from
and we look to each other

amazed at the sorrow
it is as if the world and all

its forms were burned down
and only the bones were left

shining, when I feel your skin
beside me

rising into what only we can fill—
grateful and amazed
—PETER LEVITT

Naming opens a pathway for the imagination to speak to you. Each name is part of its unique symbolic language and draws you closer to what lies beneath the surface of your life. It is like an arrow pointing homeward that says *Follow me!* Hopefully, the leaps your writing made as you discovered the hidden significance of your name was a cause for great excitement and joy. When you imbue your world with meaning, you can experience a profound and satisfying connection with your deepest self.

The creation of meaning is something you do every day to help make sense of the world. Days after a close friend of mine separated from his wife, he was looking out the window at a bougainvillea he had planted during the first months of their marriage. Like many other parts of their home, the plant suffered from neglect and was virtually bare. "Ten years," he told me. "That's what the bougainvillea meant to me. Ten years of struggling to survive." But as he looked at the plant in bitterness, he noticed something he had not seen in his desolate mood that made him happy. He told me he even felt as if the plant had suddenly surrounded itself with a spiritual light. "There was one red leaf still living," he said. "Only one. It was caught by a little breeze and was twirling from the top of an upper vine. And when I saw it, I knew without question that nothing could steal all the joy and beauty from the world."

Often, the symbols we create in our work or discover in the world are repositories of feeling. They unlock memories and experiences we have forgotten. On one occasion when I was a young man, I described the shadows beneath my grandmother's eyes and combined this description with imagery about the hard candies she kept in a small dish. The shadows were like permanent wounds, and the dish sat forgotten in an unlighted corner of her living room. The combination of these images perfectly symbolized the claustrophobia and despair I felt as a child when visiting her home. Since the writing came spontaneously—I had never seen the connection between the candies and her eyes before—I was taken entirely by surprise and suddenly, against all reason, I found myself in tears for the sad immigrant life of this woman. And within *that* sorrow I discovered another more personal sorrow of my own. This is how even the simplest symbols can hold multiple layers of meaning and emotion.

When we explore the significance of symbols that arise in such a personal and spontaneous way—and, again, this includes images that suddenly catch our eye in the world—it is similar to unraveling dream images. We feel compelled to follow them from external details to the source of meaning within. The exercises in this chapter will help you to do just that. They will guide you beneath the surface of personal and cultural symbols to the essence of what you are: *the bones beneath the bones.*

∾

For many years I kept a quotation—*"The similarity between poets and idiots is so complete it needs no comment"*—pinned to the wall above my desk to help me remember that even when I thought I knew what I was about, I didn't. This truth has always helped my writing and spiritual life to stay more closely on track. Fortunately, those times when I forgot this simple yet essential truth and started to believe my own subconscious gossip, life had a way of bringing me back to reality with a well-placed blow.

I love the sensibility of this quotation, which was given to me as a birthday present by a friend who, sadly, never wrote down the source. I read it with relief. And even though I had looked at it for the better part of ten years before misplacing it when I moved, it gave me a good laugh of recognition every time. We are what we are, after all, even if the fearful part of our psyche doesn't know exactly what that is. But *what is it? What are we?*

Knowing that we don't know is a good start. As I've said, a naked mind that engages the world yet refrains from locking it up in its metaphorical fist and declaring it *"Mine!"* is a great and essential asset for any seeker. Given the world's enormity, it reveals a modest disposition that keeps us real. When His Holiness the Dalai Lama says, "I am just a simple monk," or when Mother Teresa said, "I am not a saint. I am only tending to Christ in all his distressing disguises," the healthy relationship between a modest *not knowing* and reality is clear. It makes possible the deep knowing we need in order to truly understand the world.

I have been looking at the shapes of things and wonder-

ing what worlds they hold for as long as I can recall. As a child
I learned that this is an important way of nourishing my intuition. My father kept a few anatomy books for artists in a
drawer in the living room of our apartment, and these books
meant so much to me that after he died they were about the
only things of his I wanted for myself. The covers of these
oversize books were soft, the drawings and titles printed in a
shade of light brown very close to the color of my father's skin.
This may be one reason my childhood mind made such a
strong connection between the books and the man.

Often, between the ages of four and eight, I'd take out
these books and spend a half hour or so sitting on the floor as
I studied the detailed drawings of the human form they contained. Page after page were filled with renderings of muscles,
ligaments, tendons, skulls, eye sockets, cheek- and jawbones,
the pelvis, and the skeletal structures of shoulders, arms,
hands, legs, and feet. I had watched in amazement as my
father had made his own anatomical drawings in pencil or
charcoal, or sculpted the shapes of human heads, torsos, and
busts. Observing the care he gave to each thing as he worked
is among my earliest memories. *"Only look and you'll see that
the world is precious; its mysteries will fill you with awe"* is part
of what I took to be the meaning of how he approached his
art. Sometimes after a period of his silent looking I would
even hear him whisper to himself, "Is that so?" It was as if one
of life's mysteries had made itself known to his quiet eyes. I
knew the contents of those books had some relationship to
what my father so clearly loved to do, but I didn't know precisely what that relationship was.

One day, when I was about seven, I asked him. He was sitting across the room from me peeling an apple with the same pocketknife he used to whittle the miniature wooden animals he would later paint and put in the bedroom my brother and I shared. The man's hands and artistic patience were his genius, and I loved to watch him work.

"Pop," I said, "why do you draw the bones?" I was looking at a drawing of the human skeleton in one of his books.

"Well," he drew out in his classic way, his voice deep and strong, "if I know where the bones are, and how everything connects, I know what the skin should look like. If you know what's going on underneath the surface of things, you can figure out the rest pretty easily." And then he gave me that wink of his, and smiled.

Young as I was, the statement hit home. I could tell by the way he spoke that this was something he wanted his son to understand, though years passed before I was able to interpret its larger meaning. I started looking at things differently after that, except I'd do it in reverse. Instead of knowing what was going on inside and how it all connected, which at my young age would have been a difficult task, I'd begin with the outside and try to work my way in. I even began to imagine I had a kind of X-ray vision when I'd look at someone's face; I'd stop seeing the skin and see only the bones of the skull. If that person was talking or eating, my imagination would expose the unhinged lower jaw moving up and down. Or, because like most children I spent a lot of time playing on the floor, I'd look at the slight exposure of ankle or leg beneath my mother's or some neighbor's skirt and instead of stopping my gaze at

the color and texture of her skin, I'd picture the muscle, liga-
ment, and bone. These parts of the human body were drawn
so beautifully in my father's books, with such an abundance of
delicate shading and crosshatching lines, it was fairly easy for
me to imagine that beneath their skin the people I studied
looked just like the drawings.

As I grew older this approach to imagining what lay
beneath the world I could see joined my growing childhood
intuition about the world I couldn't see, the world of spirit and
emotion where I had come to suspect life really lived. It helped
me to gain some insight into the more subtle shades of what
people felt and why they acted as they did. It helped me to see
the world in actual *and* symbolic terms. Imagery became an
important carrier of meaning; the slightest gesture ignited my
imagination with possibility. But the fact that there were so
many possibilities was as confusing as it was enticing, and I
often stayed up at night trying to sort things out. How could I
be sure what something meant? Would I ever, finally, know?
Many artists and mystics undergo an initiation of this order at
some point in their lives. It sharpens our intuition and forges
the other tools we need to get said what must be said, to do
what we must do. It provides us with a healthy respect for
wonder and uncertainty. For *knowing nothing* at all.

It was during this time I first encountered an image of
such singular and mysterious power I could not let it alone; it
was the image of the crucified Christ. Of course, I am not the
only one who has found this image provocative, but because I
was not raised in the Christian faith each unexpected viewing
of it set my imagination wild with those Aristotelian attributes

of tragedy: pity and awe. To tell the truth, I also experienced enormous confusion as I tried to understand the intricacies of how, who, what, and why. But no matter how hard I tried, I had no way to truly comprehend such mysteries. All I had was the gift from my father: the ability to look patiently at what was before my eyes and to imagine what might lie beneath.

Over the years I have encountered many interpretations of the Crucifixion and the cross, each one explaining their significance in the life of "God made flesh." One teaching that has stayed with me says that the form of the wooden cross itself expresses a primordial relationship between the human and the Divine. The ability for a symbol as simple as two crossed lines to carry such profound significance will come into play later in this chapter when I ask you to draw and work with a personal symbol expressive of your relationship, or nonrelationship, to the Divine. To whet your appetite, let me say that almost everyone who does this exercise is moved by what it reveals. To assist your ability to do it, however, I'd like to continue exploring the cross as a template for discovering symbolic meaning within a form.

According to this teaching, the horizontal beam of the cross represents the entirety of the physical world. If you follow the horizontal line beyond the limit of the wooden beam, as if it were a beam of pure energy, it becomes a horizon without end that extends throughout space and time until it encircles and metaphorically represents all elements of the physical world. The teaching says that even in the time of his greatest suffering, as Jesus lay with his arms outstretched along this horizon, he was symbolically extending his embrace to the world. As you may know, the Christian tradition holds that the physical world of our daily lives is the relative world brought about by humankind's fall from paradise. It is the world of original sin, the foundation of human suffering and pain. The symbolic promise of Christ's outstretched arms on the wooden cross is the promise of salvation from sin, of transcendent redemption, of life everlasting for all who are encircled within that embrace.

The teaching goes on to say that while the vertical beam of the cross may appear to be physically rooted in the earth, it is spiritually rooted in the Divine. Like the horizontal beam, it extends far beyond the limits of the wooden cross, and, since it begins with the Divine, as a pathway *to* the Divine, the vertical beam represents pure spirit, the world of the absolute, which God has extended to human beings from the very beginning.

In the place where the horizon of the physical world intersects with the eternal world of the transcendent Divine, Jesus is found, embodying the promise of divine redemption, *through him,* for all other human beings.

The combination of this image and the interpretation I received is a powerful example of symbol making. It brings form, language, and intuition together in a way that leads to profound spiritual understanding. Of course, since meaning is always constructed, created by context, we cannot say in some definitive way if this interpretation is *true.* But true or not, when we allow our spiritual insight to be led by our imagination, we come closer to the essence beneath the skin of things. Moving closer clearly serves our creative needs.

A careful look at this interpretation reveals Christianity's strong foundation in the promise of transcendence. This promise imbues the figure of the cross with its particular meaning. Since in other traditions transcendence is not a prominent concept, their drawing of the nature of reality would be quite different. For example, the Zen tradition does not find a permanent distinction between what we dualistically call *spirit* and *matter*. It mostly refrains from incorporating into its forms of expression any emphasis on duality. This is why when a Zen master was asked, *"What is Buddha?"* she answered, *"Three pounds of rice!"* And when Zen master Unmon was asked, *"What is the Way?"* he replied, *"Your ordinary mind, that is the Way!"* Clearly, a simple line drawing depicting this view might be quite different from the cross. In fact, the classic Zen circle, pronounced *enso* in Japanese, is one of the primary symbols of Zen.

Versions of this belief in embodiment, or immanence, have been found in many parts of the world. When I see pictographs from some of these traditions, I know that while I am looking at a depiction of a horse, or a fish, or a bowl, or perhaps moving water or wind, I am also seeing the artist's representation of the people's belief that the Source of Life is found in everything.

As the Sufi expression says:

> *Gaze with Opened eyes at the forms you see,*
> *But go beyond, Beyond, and see the all as God.*

Before moving to the exercise, I'd like to bring in an anecdote I love. It conveys how an entire worldview can be symbolically embodied within three lines. Years ago, while I was visiting the high school my daughter attended, her English teacher approached me and said, "You know, Sheba wrote quite an essay on her spiritual beliefs."

"Really?" I said. "I didn't notice her working on it."

"Oh, that's because it was an assignment I gave in class yesterday."

"Boy, I'd love to see it," I said. "Is it very long?"

Her teacher just laughed. "No. Rather the opposite."

Uh, oh, I thought, feeling a little twinge of wonder at what my wonderful daughter had done. "How long is it?" I asked, though with typical parental anxiety I wasn't sure I really wanted to know.

"Three lines," her teacher said. "But three very good lines. I'll tell them to you, because I think you'll find them very interesting."

She then told me what my daughter had written:

> *God is above everything.*
> *The Goddess protects everything.*
> *And Buddha is everything.*

"Wow," I said. "That covers a lot of ground."

"It does, indeed," her teacher laughed, "but, after all, she is the daughter of a poet." And she gave my daughter an A.

To begin this exercise, please take out a sheet of blank paper and something you like to use for drawing or writing. When you have cleared a workspace, breathe quietly and look at the clarity of empty space the paper provides. I suggest you look at this blankness for a minute or so and mindfully follow your breath as you do. This will create the kind of solid, quiet presence your body and mind will find most beneficial for the exercise at hand.

When your concentration feels soft and light, please make a simple line drawing that expresses your current relationship to Spirit, to Source, to the Divine, however you imagine it to be. Use as much or as little of the page as you like. Your way is the right way when doing creative work. Whether your intuition of the relationship between spirit and matter lies closer to those traditions that favor notions of transcendence or those that embrace embodiment, or possibly another view I have not mentioned, please just make your drawing. Even if you have no particular belief in the Divine, or Spirit, or God, or anything at all, I think you will find this exercise of great benefit. It will help you to express your relationship to Nothing, where you will encounter the depth of your feeling and belief as well as the tributaries that stream from this belief into all parts of your life.

From time to time in my workshops, writers who hear this first instruction find the prospect of making a spontaneous though simple drawing a bit daunting. If you feel this way, please know that it is just one of your hungry ghosts starting to grumble because you are being asked to do something new. There is no need to give it any attention at all. As you may know, writing and drawing are centered in different parts of the brain, and for those who habitually rely on the language center to access their deepest self, allowing the visual center to have its say stimulates the intuition in a way that brings important surprises. The imagination listens and responds differently depending on the nature of the stimuli, and so there are great riches in store when you approach your imagination through a door that usually remains closed. Besides, after you draw you will get to write.

In the fourteenth century, the Sufi master Hafiz wrote:

> *You need to become a pen*
> *In the Sun's hand.*
>
> *We need for the earth to sing*
> *Through our pores and eyes.*
>
> *The body will again become restless*
> *Until your soul paints all its beauty*
> *Upon the sky.*

It is our good fortune that each of us instinctively knows how to be the pen, the vessel through which the earth may sing as our true self joyfully, *joyfully,* paints all its beauty upon the sky. This instinct is part of the miracle of being what we are; we don't have to depend upon any special talents or skills. To paraphrase Kazuaki Tanahashi, there is no need to imagine before you make your drawing. Drawing brings forth imagination. It is as easy for us to give voice to this instinct as it is for the spring frogs to sing their mating songs along the length of the stream that runs through our land on its way to the lake. (Which they are doing right now, and loud!) This is doing what we know before we know what we do. All we need is to lift the pen and begin.

After you have made your drawing, please put your pen or pencil down and look at what you've drawn as the new thing it is. Accept it. There is nothing to judge or understand here. It is just a simple line or a series of lines that stem from some intuitive sense you have about yourself and your spiritual life.

As you look at what you have drawn, allow yourself to become interested in one particular part of the drawing. Perhaps it will be a place where lines cross, or the center of a spiral, or you might choose the blank space outside of your drawing at the edge of the page as your point of focus. Wherever it is, please look at it quietly and then, maintaining the spirit of spontaneity, write down on the drawing itself one word that expresses what you feel this part of the drawing says. For example, while looking at her drawing, one woman noticed she had made a dot at the top of a series of lines that cascaded down the page. Suddenly it became clear to her what this dot represented in her own spiritual life; beside it she wrote the word *Beginning*. It can be as simple and quick as that. Notice how a dot might have inspired a different response in you. As I have said, each of our drawings is a symbolic language of a highly personal nature. Please look at one part of your drawing quietly and write any word that comes to you.

Once you have done this, repeat the process two more times with two other parts of your drawing, taking care to engage each new location with a fresh, quiet, accepting mind.

As you do you may discover that a particular sensation of freedom accompanies your act. It is the joy of creative release. Allow yourself to enjoy not knowing where these words come from and why they are coming to you right now. Be curious. Be puzzled. You may even be amazed.

Remember, it may appear that you are speaking when you write these words beside your drawing, but in reality you are simply writing down what you are being told from some deep part of yourself that wants you to know. It's a bit like hearing whatever it is my father saw just prior to his whispering, "Is that so?" Listening deeply is essential to all creative acts, even the ones we seem to do in a flash. What ignites that flash has been with us for a long time, and when we finally do act, we get to discover what has been going on underground, so to speak. A small amount of light illuminates a large, dark room.

The work you have done thus far has not only brought you a drawing and three words, it has also brought you closer to knowing something profound about yourself at this moment of your life. Please take your three words to a blank sheet of paper and write them at the top. As you look at your words, allow them to speak to each other. Let them spark your intuition—and when they do, follow wherever it leads. This is an opportunity for you to give voice to the symbolic significance of your drawing and the language it called forth. If you like, begin by placing just two of your words beside each other to see what spontaneous images, feelings, or memories they inspire. Take your time as you engage these words. Let your intuition come into play as you seek to express the meaning their combination has brought about. Then do it again until you have used all the possible combinations.

One student's drawing of her relationship to the Divine inspired her to write the words *empty, love,* and *going.* As she combined the words two at a time she was met with one surprise after another. Phrases like *empty love, empty going, going empty, a going love,* and other combinations created a window into what she had previously known only as a vague sense of being spiritually discouraged. She had never been able to name it. As she wrote, the amorphous feelings that had been calling to her for years flew onto the page. One image after another set these feelings free.

After you have worked with your words in combinations of two, work with all three words at one time. The various connections your words make as you begin to write will help you to give even greater expression to what your imagination wants you to understand. Please give yourself over completely to your writing. Write as if you were a pen in the Sun's hand. Write as the Sun itself. You may be as serious or as playful in doing this as you like. No matter which approach you choose, these words will tell you something new, something that has stirred in your body or mind, seeking release. Let these words hold the pen awhile and draw you into an act of writing that will help you discover the shape of a spiritual expression entirely your own. In this way your writing will make a drawing of you, rooted in the bones beneath the bones that support your life.

In doing this exercise and the ones that follow keep it simple, keep it real. *"Your ordinary mind, that is the Way!"* Our ability to find our own shape and paint our deepest selves upon the sky is as natural to us as taking a breath. *Only look! Only listen! Only breathe!* Then write for as long as you like.

As you have just discovered, personal symbols and images are rooted in our own authentic ground. They mean what they mean because we say they do. They need no other authority than this. When we trace them to their source, we make it possible for elements of our deepest self to be named. But symbols of an archetypal or cultural origin can also provide the opportunity for our most intimate selves to be known. In part, this is because they work on our imagination from an angle that is quite different from those personally derived. Our knowledge or history with such symbols affect our responses when they are encountered. Sometimes we are not aware of what makes us respond as we do, but we feel a definite visceral reaction. Some symbols draw us in while others push us away. Each of these reactions contains significant personal truths our writing will reveal.

The following exercises will give you an opportunity to use some of the techniques you've used above to discover the personal meaning of an archetypal image. They will also introduce you to other methods you will find of enormous use as you engage such symbols in your life. The origin of these exercises comes from a dream in which I was gazing into an absolutely beautiful, deep-blue sky. There wasn't a cloud in sight, and by some mystical and invisible means, the color of the sky felt as if it visually echoed the depth of my own heart, which yearned upward with great feeling toward that perfect blue. Just looking at the color of the sky transported me as if it was my first sighting of the Beloved. But even more remarkable was the fact that I suddenly saw, floating in the middle of that sky, a huge, golden, six-pointed star, known in the Jewish tradition as the Magen David, or Star of David. The sight of the star astonished me, of course, but what took my breath away completely was the appearance of golden words floating beside each point of the star. There was one word for each point, and they shone with the same mystical glow as the star itself.

As I beheld this vision in my dream, my mouth opened in awe and my body became as weightless as light. Then, with a sensation of deep longing that seemed to lift my heart right out from where it nested beneath my ribs, I saw that the words surrounding the star spelled out in Hebrew one of the most sacred of Jewish prayers, known as the Shema: *"Shema Yisrael Adonai Eloheinu Adonai Echad."*

For now I'd like to offer a fairly common translation of this prayer, which Jewish people are asked to say at various times in their lives but most especially just before the moment of death: *"Hear, Israel, the Lord Is God, the Lord Is One."*

I was standing there looking at this extraordinary sight with a clear sense of eternity permeating my body and mind when suddenly a voice said to me: *This is a teaching from the women.* As if on cue, the golden letters of the prayer began to undulate until they transformed into wisps of smoke that rose like incense ghosts high into the blue sky above the golden star. I watched as the letters of each word lost their form, ascended, and disappeared.

Then I woke up, and I mean *up!*

I sat in my bed in the dark for a few minutes, startled, thrilled, disturbed, trying to recall every detail of my dream and completely mystified by what the voice had told me. *"This is a teaching from the women."* What could I make of it all? It was so vivid and strange.

I turned on my light, and there beside me was a book I had been studying before going to bed. I opened it to where I last had read and found a story about Beruria, the wife of Rabbi Meir, who felt that her husband was mistaken to pray that those who had done wicked deeds should perish from the Earth. Beruria believed in the basic goodness of people and told her husband that he should pray for sinners to regret their actions and change their ways because then sinfulness itself would be eradicated, not the human beings who sin.

As I pondered this story, and my dream, seeking the intuitive pathway between them, I began to suspect that Beruria may have understood the meaning of the last word of the prayer, *Echad,* in a way that revolutionized my own understanding. Perhaps this word did not simply mean "One," as in "one God," but *"Oneness."* Suddenly I felt as if for the first time I could feel the meaning of this holy prayer: *Hear! That which you know of as God, the Infinite, the Unnamable Unifying Source of All Creation, is Oneness itself!*

I don't think it is too far-fetched to say that the teaching from the women is that since the nature of the Source of Life is Oneness, no person who sins (a fairly common definition of sin is to be at a distance from God, or Oneness—and who is not at any given moment?) should be removed from the circle of creation and life. Rather, all people whose words and deeds cause them to be separated from this Source should do their best to return, and to help others to return, to the origin from which the creation was born.

As Beruria's teaching and the image of the star intermingled in my mind, I grew sleepy again and began to visualize the words of the prayer circling the star endlessly, eternally. They were like planets slowly orbiting the Sun. This reminded me of the teaching that the Creator and all things of creation were inseparably unified. Though the nature of this relationship may not always be apparent, the teaching says they are one. I had always found this sensibility a powerful force in my life as a writer. It was the source of my confidence in the imagination's ability to offer what most nourished my writing as a vehicle for returning me to One. After a while I turned out my reading lamp and fell into a deep sleep with this very thought in mind. In the morning, the following exercise came to me, and I wrote it down.

Please take out a sheet of paper no smaller than ordinary typing paper, though it may be as large as you like. Whatever size you choose, I'd like you to consider this paper to be as expansive as the heavens in my dream. In this way you will already engage your imagination in a field it finds most familiar, most real. Take a few moments to breathe quietly to settle yourself before your own blue sky, and when you have, please draw a six-pointed star on the paper before you. Be sure to make your star a good, substantial size, but leave a bit of room beside each of its points.

In one of his books, *The Jew in the Lotus,* Rodger Kamenetz tells us that the six-pointed star has quite a surprising history. It originated in Mesopotamia as a symbol of fertility but was brought to India by the Aryans, where it came to represent Shakti, the mother. Later on Tantric Buddhism used this figure as a symbol of the cervix, and in the late Middle Ages it served as a Jewish symbol, representing the shield of David the King. It seems this star has always expressed a primary, even primordial, connection to either the creation or protection of life.

After you have drawn your star, please sit quietly and return your attention to your breath. Again, working with your breath while doing creative work—or *any* kind of work—keeps you centered and aids your concentration. In fact, the word *concentration* means "with a center." When you are aware of your breathing during any activity you quickly become grounded, focused, and clear. This awareness also gives a measure of rest and ease to your body and mind while you work, which keeps them vulnerable, like the permeable membranes we want them to be. Then, whether you are asleep or awake, you are able to more fully experience the contents of your imagination and dreams.

The next part of this exercise is called *conscious dreaming.* Take a look at the space surrounding the star you have drawn. At first it may seem to be just empty space. It may appear silent. Often, when we start to write, we greet the blankness of a page with a certain hesitation or fear. But I ask you to consider that just as the primordial silence contains within itself the potential for all articulation, all written words and speech, the silent space before you is already filled with your own possibilities. As you breathe quietly and become more at ease while gazing at your star, begin to imagine that there are many letters, many words, and even many worlds already there at each point of the star. Each of these is waiting to be discovered.

Turn your attention to the topmost point of the star, and imagine a letter starting to emerge from the blank page like a photographic image that rises out of the developing fluid. This is similar to what you did when working with your personal drawing, except that there you started by writing whole words. The letter may be in Hebrew, if you are acquainted with that language, or in English. If you are familiar with another language, feel free to work with it. Just allow whatever letter that wants to come to you to emerge out of the page. Without thinking about the particular letter at all, or wondering what it may mean, please write it beside the topmost point of your star.

Now move to the first point of your star to the right and repeat the process. Remember to breathe calmly and easily as you do this, allowing the letter to float up out of the fabric of the page just like the words in my dream floated out of the endlessness of the clear blue sky. Whatever letter appears, meet it without any judgment at all. When you withhold judgment it gives permission to your entire creative process to offer itself freely to you, so be generous and welcome whatever wants to make itself known.

After you have repeated this process with the first point to the right, do the same at each of the other points of the star.

You may find that it helps if you write the letter each time on the exhale of your breath. This creates a spacious feeling inside you as you express the unknown. Since we are more vulnerable when we exhale, it is a good way to feel the aliveness of being curious and amazed. When you have completed working at the remaining four points, please put down your pencil, pen, or crayon and calmly look at your star. Become interested in your letters, as if you've never seen them before. What could it all mean?

It's too early to ask this question.

When you are ready, go around the star again beginning with the topmost point and write beside each point a word that begins with the letter you have just written. Remember to repeat the process of consciously breathing and dreaming while you write, allowing for the surprise of whatever wants to appear. If at the top of your star you find the letter *B*, you might write *Beginning*, or *Birth*, or *Blessing*, or *Bat*. If the letter to the right of that is *S*, you might write *Sister*, or *Suchness*, or *Slave*. Or you might choose to write someone's name for one of your words. Whatever words you write should be authentically rooted in your life.

There is a powerful relationship between authenticity and permission. They reinforce each other's activity like elements of a Möbius strip. They also foster spontaneity. Allen Ginsberg used to encourage spontaneous expression by saying, *"First thought, best thought."* This is always sound, liberating advice. When you give yourself permission to go forward with work you truly mean, you gain the upper hand over any negative inner criticism that may arise. Such criticism is just no match for the powerful combination of authenticity, permission, and spontaneity. If, as you do this exercise, a voice rises up that tries to cast doubt on the words you choose, or the exercise, or your ability to do it, or what it all means, just take a breath, smile inside yourself at that voice, and then *go back to work*. Once again, this is just a hungry ghost trying to steal your attention because it feels your imagination starting to stir as you engage the unknown. The most important thing now is that you allow yourself to work with a feeling of ease and discovery as these new words make themselves known to you.

After you have written down the six words, please read them over and allow them to begin to circulate inside you. Let them spark each other, or become magnets that draw each other closer. Let them show you intuitive connections you never saw before. Do this for no more than a minute and then do some freewriting for fifteen or twenty minutes, using all of the words and any associations, images, memories, or feelings they bring to mind. You might notice that some of the words want to get closer to each other because they seem to go well together, or you might notice some of them eyeing each other suspiciously because they do not seem to relate to each other at all. Go ahead and explore each of these situations in separate pieces. As you do, remember to grant yourself the same spirit of discovery, permission, and ease you felt when the letters and words emerged. Let this spirit permeate you as you write. *And write whatever you like!*

After you have done the freewriting exercise described above, you may take a break or you may move on. When you start to work, take a look at the star. The upward-facing triangle, whose single point is at the top of the star, has been associated with human beings who stand firmly on Earth while casting their gaze upward toward the Divine. Please notice the words you have *already* written at the three points of this triangle and write them down on a fresh sheet of paper.

The downward-facing triangle, whose single point is the lowest point of your star, has been associated with the Divine looking from the heavens toward us on Earth. Please notice the words you have written at the three points of this triangle and write these down on a separate, fresh sheet of paper.

The next part of this exercise consists of your considering the words in each of these triangles. Working with one set of words at a time, please write for fifteen or twenty minutes, using these words as starting points, or sparks, as you consider the thoughts, feelings, associations, intuitions, and images of your relationship to the Divine or what you feel is the Divine's relationship to you. Please remember your writing will be based on the words you have already written, though this time you may choose not to use the actual words in your writings.

Sometimes the words that have come to you may immediately lead to natural discoveries and revelations and the writing will just take off. Sometimes you may find yourself mystified by how these words could possibly express anything about the relationship between you and the Infinite Creator, the Divine. In either case, please trust the clarity of your intuitive imagination and begin to write. Remember, all beginnings are places where the negative judge likes to throw you off track. If this starts to occur, just give it another brief smile, take a breath, and plunge into your writing.

This part of the exercise gives you a chance to use the content your imagination has provided so you may realize spiritual beliefs and yearnings you may never have expressed before. Despite the fact that the source of your words is an image derived externally, the root of your writing is your own spontaneous mind. The words that came to you in the very beginning of this exercise are part of your own intuitive understanding of yourself in direct relation to the symbol you were given. When we accept these words and permit them enough space and time to show us what they want us to know, the expression that results is always very true, very strong.

In his discussion of the diverse cultural meanings of the star, Rodger Kamenetz makes clear that at different times in its history elements of what have been called the *masculine* and the *feminine* have been emphasized. When it represented the shield of King David, he says, *"it was what one thrusts out to the world as a mark of identity."* A masculine image if ever I've heard one. Tantric Buddhism's understanding of the star as a cervix leads us in the other direction. As *"an esoteric part of the body, hidden within, a mystery, the neck of the womb, the channel through which all life emerges . . . [it] is purely and uniquely feminine."* I find both interpretations provocative and have found a way to work with the star to explore the connection between our spiritual and sexual lives.

The downward-pointing triangle is a universal symbol of

what C. G. Jung referred to as the *feminine archetype*. This symbol has been found in many parts of the world in cultural artifacts dating back to the earliest human civilizations. In the Jewish tradition it has been related to the Shechinah, sometimes called the feminine aspect of the Divine. The upward-pointing triangle has been seen as representing the *masculine archetype* because of its phallic, upward-thrusting formation.

With the symbolic gender orientation of the two triangles in mind, take a look at the words you have already written around each form. This is occasionally the time in workshops when people laugh out loud with recognition or shake their heads hopelessly. How do the words fit the form for you? Do they seem perfect? Crazy? Challenging? Ridiculous? All of these might be true.

No matter what you think of them, or the connections they do or do not seem to make, please give yourself sufficient time to work with each constellation of words and, once again, allow them to speak in a fresh piece of writing based on where these words and gender orientations lead you. I promise there is a great surprise waiting for you as you enter the personal and archetypal sexual mystery held within the components of the star.

Before we leave the star, let me remind you that all the writing you have just completed was based on a single image appearing in one dream—a dream that was not even your own. But as you have hopefully just discovered, things can become our own when we make them so. This is one of the reasons we find particular paintings and poems so compelling. Their imagery and symbols speak to us in a highly personal way, and cause such powerful self-recognition that they seem to have arisen from the deepest ground of our own true selves.

Many times the kind of mirroring I find in another artist's work makes the world in which I stand seem to fall away. I feel plunged into a silence of great profundity, though there is no sense of isolation at all. Quite the opposite. I feel gratitude to the artist for his or her ability to make me transparent to myself, and I feel connected to something so large that life streams through me with undeniable clarity and force. It is an experience very close to prayer.

THE RIDDLE
OF HANDS

☾

I saw myself
a ring of bone
in the clear stream
of all of it

and vowed,
always to be open to it
that all of it
might flow through

and then heard
"ring of bone" where
ring is what a

bell does
      —LEW WELCH

In Western religious tradition it is said that when we die we stand naked before God. It is the moment when all we have become is reflected back to us through God's eyes and we can finally see what we have made of our lives. The tradition holds that this is the most highly magnified moment of exposure we will ever face. But when a writer sits before the blankness of a page and then begins to write, or when a painter stands in silence before the empty canvas and then sweeps the brush forward to make her mark, the naked reflection that appears is also powerful in the extreme. It is a similar moment of truth.

As I wrote at the end of the previous chapter, when writers or artists express such truth, their work makes it possible for me to recognize in myself what I had not seen before. When this occurs I feel such a strong bond with them that I seek to know more about their lives; in particular, what roots them in their work and imagination. Henri Matisse was one painter whose spiritual and sensual expression flowed powerfully through his brush into color and form. As I looked at his paintings during one period of my life, I wanted to know what ground he stood on and set off to see what I could find. I was not disappointed. *"The essential thing,"* he wrote, *"is to work in a state of mind that approaches prayer."* It is a statement I loved from the start. It points unwaveringly to a quality of naked relationship, of eros in its truest sense, between our deepest selves, our world, and our creative lives. Embracing the spacious clarity of this state of mind as we write nourishes and strengthens our ability to express the truth of what we are.

Lew Welch, whose poem appears at the start of this chapter, was an American poet committed to a prayerful heart and mind, though there was nothing traditionally religious about him. He worshiped in the forests and streams of the North American West. His fellow congregants were poets, badgers, eagles, and bears. In a piece called "The Riddle of Hands," Lew reminds us that throughout the history of the world, in each place and at all times as far as we can track it, there has been a spiritual tradition in which people have brought their hands together in what has become known in many cultures as the gesture of prayer. People do this in order to signify that something of moment is occurring, something that causes them to make this spontaneous gesture of reverence as an expression of their unified body and mind: their spirit, one might say. Often, when we feel we are in the presence of the sacred, we bring our hands together before our heart to express gratitude or awe. At other times our hands may come together to express the moment when we most deeply seek the kind of intimacy prayer can provide. Sometimes we bring our hands together and close our eyes to more fully experience what has touched us. There are also times when we open our eyes wide and clasp our hands together in joy.

Whether we express ourselves with this gesture spontaneously or because we have been taught, the joining together of our hands signifies a kind of intimate touching or connection. It expresses the end of distance between what we usually see as ourselves and what lies right before us, whether it is a person, an experience of joy or gratitude, or some feeling of contact with our deepest self that we cannot yet name.

In the moment our left and right hands are brought

together to form one point before our heart, it is not too difficult to experience the oneness this symbol represents. I'd like
you to explore this gesture to see what it holds. Bring your
hands together slowly with some sensitivity and awareness. As
you do, place the focus of your mind in your hands. Notice
how you are actually coming closer to yourself, traveling that
distance from separateness to intimacy you may not have
known was right there in your own life. Please do this with
care several times. How do you feel as your hands approach
each other and finally touch? It is not uncommon to experience a deep satisfaction as this gesture is made, almost as if
one has come home.

This coming together of your hands acknowledges the
oneness of their world. We can also use this gesture to represent the ending of other dualities whose real, interdependent
nature has been misunderstood. Imagine for a moment that
you hold good and bad, right and wrong, and self and other in
your hands as you bring them closer together and let them
finally touch. It can be quite powerful to experience, or at
least to imagine, those separate lives returning to the one
ground from which all life comes. In doing so we conceptually
satisfy a personal and universal longing that Allen Ginsberg
expressed so movingly in his poem "Song":

> *yes, yes,*
> > *that's what*
> *I wanted,*
> > *I always wanted,*
> > *I always wanted,*

> *to return*
>
> *to my body*
>
> *where I was born*

As you bring your hands together, notice how native to your body this gesture really does feel. Observe how it does not come to you from the outside but is as natural to you as breathing, expressive of what you already are and know. Notice how your head lowers as you do this, perhaps even your eyelids. This is no cultural artifact. This is something we were born knowing how to do. It is, in physical form, a powerful act of return.

When people the world over offer blessings, this gesture of prayer is frequently part of the offering. That is no coincidence. Blessing draws us closer and helps us to become intimate with what we bless. The act of blessing makes the people or objects of our devotional wishes real for us in a way they weren't before. It causes them to rise newly seen in our imagination as we express our deepest intention through the blessing. And we, those offering such blessings, become real and see ourselves in a new way as well. This is because, once again, intimacy is both the root and the fruition of the act.

I think of this intimacy as a relationship of one to One. When we live and work with an attitude approaching prayer, such intimacy can't help but carry this sacred, erotic charge into what we do. It is part of what makes this prayerful gesture so potent. Every day before I begin to write, I incorporate this gesture into my work. I light a stick of incense and with quiet concentration place it into the incense burner. Then I place my hands together and offer three standing bows. I don't have any particular thoughts in mind as I do this, but I am aware that my intention is for my prayerful attitude to be felt everywhere. When we offer this act of intimate touching without touching, and do so with humility and respect, the union it creates can, if only for a moment, repair what life has broken.

Let me suggest that you practice this gesture a few times before writing. As you repeat the gesture, it is best if you avoid allowing it to become automatic. Rather, allow the intention behind the gesture to come through every time. Bring to it the sense that you are offering medicine for a world in need, a world gone mad. This will help you to remember that as you make this offering, small as you are, you are actually gathering the entirety of the world in your own two hands. The spirit with which we do this is what draws the shattered world back into one and helps us to touch our true nature, our authentic selves.

Please begin by offering this gesture to yourself. Be the one giving and the one receiving. Do this silently several times. Let the gesture enter your imagination. Do it with reverence. When this reverence permeates your experience, walk slowly around your room while maintaining this gesture with your hands. Notice how walking with this prayerful gesture, and breathing quietly, changes how you feel and see as you walk. If you like, you can bow to the floor you stand upon, the floor that supports you. When you do this you are bowing to the floor, to the ground, and to the ground beneath the ground. Why not offer a bow to that which really supports us?

Once you have made this bow, please keep walking and allow your eye to be caught by something: your chair, for example, the one you sit on when you write, or your desk. You might also choose a flower in a vase, or a photograph you keep near you. Anything. Everything. After all, each thing your eye rests upon is an element of your daily life as you live it, which includes your creative and spiritual life. These lives cannot be separated. If you look deeply enough at the objects in your room and consider what role they play, what practical and symbolic value they hold, you will surely find something of sacred relationship to yourself and your world in each of them. This is not just poetic wishful thinking. The sacred and the practical are also One. But you must look. Seen properly, there is nothing that does not receive this bow. How about the cup that holds your pencils and pens, or the air conditioner? Even the air conditioner may receive this gesture and, with you, come back to One.

Please do this entire exercise now—and when you bow, I hope you will allow your head to lower a little toward your heart as an expression of surrender. Do your best to give yourself entirely away. If you bow with sincerity, you will find something waiting for you here. Perhaps you may want to walk outside and offer this bow to some trees, or a river, or the entirety of the empty sky. If you are fortunate enough to live in a place where this may be done, why wait?

After you do what I've suggested above, please offer this gesture to someone you love, or someone who has loved you. Do this as an act of imagination, as well as an expression of gratitude. See or feel that person within your own mind or heart's eye. Give yourself entirely away to whomever you choose, or to whomever comes to you when you read these words. You may be surprised who it is. One time when I did this the face of a boy I had not thought about for more than forty years came flying out of my imagination. I ask only that you come to it as nakedly as you can, in a state of mind that approaches blessing, or prayer.

Once this part is completed, please bring to mind someone with whom you have had difficulty or pain and offer a bow. Notice your reluctance to do so, but please make this offering nonetheless. You may think of someone in your family or close circle of friends, but it can just as easily be someone at work. One woman offered this prayerful bow to the thought of a man who had been quite arbitrarily unkind to her as she walked by on the street. Another used this act of imagination as the first act of return to an estranged parent. A number of people have braved the first offering by beginning with someone not particularly close to them, but then found that the act itself was so nourishing they felt encouraged to offer it to many other people in their lives. Whole lists ensued, and the experience brought about a surprising sense of freedom. It also put these people in touch with their own basic goodness. Please begin by choosing one person and offering this gesture to him now.

Finally, I ask that you offer this to the doing itself. Bow to bowing. Bow to the ability and opportunity to do so. Allow yourself to really feel the intimacy of this. Once you do, sit and breathe quietly, reverently, in the same manner as your bow, and allow yourself to feel the many feelings and notice the diverse associations the entire cycle of bowing has engendered. Then begin to write.

I suggest you write in a manner that supports and expresses the quiet, open feeling this prayerful gesture tends to bring about. Without any preset time limits in mind, follow this feeling wherever it leads and for as long as you can. When we work in this way, the product of our labor tends to convey the experience without necessarily speaking about it directly. It is a perfect example of how the quality of our being and our words can really merge into one. It is also a perfect preparation for the writing you will do in the next chapter, where the focus is prayer.

THERE ARE HUNDREDS
OF WAYS TO KNEEL
AND KISS
THE GROUND

☾

The title of this chapter comes from the great fourteenth-century Sufi poet Jalaluddin Rumi. When I first read Rumi's words, I felt the gratitude of the poet resound through my entire being. I felt the generosity of his vision and the openness of his heart. It was as if they had been transferred to me. I was thunderstruck. It shouldn't be such a mystery that a great and true line of poetry has the power to shape the moment in which it is received—this is what great writing does—but this experience was so all-pervasive, and so surprising, that I have to say I almost felt transformed into a prayer with gratitude at its heart.

I want to explore prayer from a perspective that may be quite new in the West. Afterward, when you write, I'm sure you will see how to use this teaching to creatively bring your deepest self to life. In the Sufi tradition it is taught that all things in the universe are constantly in prayer: every leaf and tree, every stone, the snowfall on every mountain, and all the night sky stars that whirl invisibly throughout the day. According to this teaching, all things seen and unseen, known and unknown, are simultaneously and constantly in prayer. When you hold a flower, or a baby, or your friend's or lover's hand, you are holding a life in prayer. I think it is fair to say the tradition also believes that when you hear a song coming from across a field—for example, a song as filled with its own beauty as the prayer of gratitude I somehow became—then singer and song and field *are prayer.* In other words, being and prayer are synonymous.

But what does it mean to "be prayer"? We normally would say that someone is *in* prayer. Or that we pray. (Notice that our usual view maintains that prayer belongs solely to the human realm.) But to be prayer? What could it mean?

This morning, as I was considering this question, I left my studio and walked through the snow-covered field that leads down to the lake. All around me, and at a great height, the pine and cedar forest held boughs weighted with great and individually shaped drifts of snow. The sky was an extraordinary blue, though that was beginning to change, and there were traces of a northern breeze in the upper branches and limbs. A new front would be coming soon. From time to time one of these boughs would almost imperceptibly sway and let the snow loose. I watched as it arced through the air with the clarity and grace of a great white heron heading down. When it landed, there was the softest of sounds.

I have written before that we cannot really take credit for the content of our spontaneous thoughts, or the direction they may take. These things just occur as an expression of the imagination's desire for us to know. And so I cannot say why, as I continued down to the lake, I found myself thinking about the night my wife spent in labor before giving birth to our son. Perhaps it has something to do with the silence of the snowy world in which I walked, so similar to what I experience as prayer.

My wife decided to begin her labor while sitting in a rocking chair. It's the position she found most comfortable as the labor came on. Since it was almost midnight, I lay on the bed near her chair and watched as she glided rhythmically back and forth until she moved more deeply into a contemplative mood. From time to time I asked how she was doing and if she needed anything, the sort of checking in you might imagine, but she said she wanted to concentrate on her breathing and remain silent awhile, and then she closed her eyes. Since this was a perfectly natural way of being for her, and I was relieved the labor had not yet progressed to the more difficult stages one could reasonably predict, I picked up a book and began to read. Of course, the warmth of the room in late November and the steady movement of the chair coupled with the quality of silence and concentration that came from the woman sitting near me, and before long all my plans to be of great assistance went out the window and I fell asleep.

I awakened somewhat surprised five hours later and found to my amazement that Shirley was still in that chair, though I could see a difference in her. I quickly brought some water and for reasons I won't go into roused her from the deep place to which she had gone. I'll let the story drop here except to say that things moved very quickly after that, and a little more than two hours later, after a quite typical and strenuous latter stage of labor, the midwife placed into Shirley's arms our new little boy.

After the birth, when we were all three alone, I asked Shirley, "Where did you go when you were meditating in the chair? You were so far gone when I awoke that it was a little hard to actually find you." "I know," she said. "I'm not exactly sure what happened, but I began to meditate, and to pray in the way that I do, and before I knew it I found I was in that place where I recognize myself."

I know her birthing experience was unusual, to say the least, and that we were fortunate, but I also know from our conversation that she entered the place where being is prayer.

The Sufi tradition, like many others, believes that we are separated from the oneness of God, the wholeness of the Divine, by a veil. Only that. It sounds so transparent, and perhaps it is if we understand that the veil is really the creation of our own perception and thought as we move through the world. To paraphrase the great English poet and engraver William Blake (I have to admit that while most of the words you are about to read are Blake's own, to quote him in paraphrase does feels like a bit of a crime): A shadow rises above us born from our wearied intellect, a sweet entrancing self-delusion, a self-consuming dark devourer that closes the circumference of our lives and darkens our center till we see all things solely through the narrow chinks of our cavern. *"Thought,"* this great poet wrote, *"changed the infinite to a serpent."*

It is difficult for us to remain in touch with the whole-ness of the Infinite given the ordinary functioning and per-spective of our mind. But the Sufis teach that we can have that self-created veil lifted and encounter the oneness of the Infi-nite by prayer. Please note I do not say that *we* lift the veil, but that the veil is lifted. Lifted by what or whom? The Sufis tell us Muhammad the Prophet taught that when our prayer encompasses our entire being, it opens a secret passageway between the one praying and the One prayed to. When this takes place, the veil is lifted by Wholeness—by Oneness itself—which we reach through prayer.

In light of this teaching, I can only admire my wife's real-ization that her prayer and meditation established a similar passageway until she found she was in that place where she recognized her self—what has been called the Big Self—where being is prayer and all things may be found.

As the stone shows, and the snowfall, and the song, and as my wife's experience shows, and perhaps experiences of your own, the veils are lifted and we can spontaneously express our true selves just as they are because of the unity of being and prayer. Isn't this exactly what Matisse and many other great artists want us to discover? Don't their paintings express this unity again and again? Isn't Rumi's poetry rooted precisely here? If these artists were able to see through appear-ances to the nature of things and express themselves fully in this way, so can we. We, too, can have the secrets of the world open before our eyes as the prayer and song of life are seen for what they are.

When we let ourselves see the constant prayer a field of summer grass makes, or the graceful bow of a sunflower ripened with seeds, we come into contact with an essence at the core of their lives that is both individual and universal. It is the essence—the fullness—found in all things where being and prayer are one. To touch this in any part of the world has a mirroring effect. Of course, this is as easily true for the natural world as it is for art. In both cases, an act of recognition occurs where we *re-cognize,* or *know again,* what we have always known, though it often slips away. In the case of being and prayer, this act of recognition awakens the prayer that resides at the core of our own being. It helps us to discover the meaning of this prayer and shows us how to bring it to life.

We should have confidence in this. We already know how to have the veil lifted. It is our nature to realize our individual and universal essence, the heart of what we are. One of the root meanings of the word *mystic* is "to close the eyes." I love this. When we quiet our mind and close our eyes to our usual way of seeing, we open them upon the larger world of our true nature. Then we can see all the secrets laid bare, including the prayer every part of our world makes with its life.

Please take this teaching on prayer with you as you write. We don't just pray to ask, though of course at times we may do that as well. We pray as a way of being. Why not test this in the world? Go outside before you write and see for yourself.

Walk in some wild part of the natural world or go to a park in the city and sit quietly while children play nearby. The teaching tells us that all things are in constant prayer. What do you observe in these places about the unity of being and prayer? What do you intuit? After you return from your walk, sit quietly in your room and write, basing your words on what you have seen. Write from within the *being-prayer* you observed. Concentrate on one form of this after another and let your writing express that life as you imagine it experiences itself. Then follow wherever your writing leads.

After you have completed this writing, please maintain the sense of presence your writing required and, once again, look around your room. Widen your investigation into being and prayer. If you have some flowers in a vase, please rely on your intuition and ask yourself, How does a flower pray? What are the elements, what is the meaning, of its prayer? What have you been living with unnoticed all along?

I ask you to consider these kinds of questions both literally and symbolically with an openness of heart and mind. Practice "closing the eyes" and intuitively reach across to what is before you in a way that is new. If you have a candle in your room, ask yourself, What is the meaning of a candle's prayer? What is its meaning before it is lit and also after the flame is burning? Does it change or remain the same? Is it possible that in some way the flame has been alive inside the life of this candle all along, like a prayer longing to be heard? Close your eyes and ask.

The relationship between longing and prayer has been experienced in the usual way by most people who have prayed. It is how we were taught and how we teach our children. But if we add to our understanding of this relationship the teaching that being is prayer, then the longing takes on a whole new meaning. Please look into this now. Sit quietly until you feel a steadiness of body and mind. When you do, look into your own depth and ask what prayer, like a flame inside a candle, is already alive. If you ask this with your whole being, you will find a treasure of great value that has lived within you all along.

After you have contemplated these matters and written in the way I've suggested, please write one more time. Write the expressive prayer of your life, seen new. Write it as a classic prayer if you like, or in poetry or prose. Write it simply as a note to yourself or as a postcard to the Infinite, but write with the intention to completely express your experience of being and prayer. As you work, please allow your writing to be the passageway, the birth canal, through which you arrive at the place where you recognize yourself. Rumi is correct. There are hundreds of ways to kneel and kiss the ground. *Each of us has hundreds of ways.* Please remember this. If you do, you will discover that in one piece after another your writing can express the vitality and truth of your life rooted in the ground of your being, your prayer.

A MATTER
OF CHANCE

☾

The more completely we give ourselves to the creative opportunities our imagination provides, the more our writing nourishes our spiritual quest. When you allow practices like the ones you worked with in the last chapter to become a consistent part of your larger inquiry, the process not only nurtures your deepest self, it also opens up pathways your imagination will use in other ways. It is a bit like hard-wiring creative receptors. Once they are set to receive, it is simply who you are. This is as true for being prayer as it is for taking a risk, cultivating naked mind, or going to the narrow place in order to help you to know and to heal. Of course, when we utilize one or more of these methods we are really only awakening an inherent capability that has been less active in the past, but each time it feels as if we have something new.

The spontaneous products of our imagination give us a window into our limitless creative nature. What may appear to be an offhand comment, a slip of the tongue, or a key struck mistakenly on the computer is really just a new way to articulate and to see. Mistakes and supposed accidents are often the unconscious humor and wisdom our psyche designs to catch our attention. We should not take such things lightly. Each one can be a crack in the wall that separates our surface lives from our truer selves.

The spirit we bring to our work can either promote the discovery of such openings or shut them down. For example, if over time we repeat the exercises in this book as if we are merely repeating what we've done before, our attitude causes us to miss the opportunity for them to take us somewhere new. If you say you already know what a flower is—and thereby substitute the concept for the living thing —you miss the chance to see and know the flower before you now. It is the same with spiritual and creative practices. You may appear to be doing the same old thing, but in truth there is no "same old thing"; there is only *this* thing, and *this you*, now.

This is easily seen when it comes to chanting. I love to chant. I love the full engagement of body and mind it depends upon. I love how the repeated vocalization lets me enjoy in my own voice how many ways there are to articulate the vowels. I love the sensations that run through me as chanting awakens my body's rhythmic pulse. I love how this makes me start to move and how such movement integrates all parts of myself until my linear, rational mind surrenders to one that I experience as more naked and clear. When we give ourselves entirely to the repetition of the chant it creates a powerful sense of presence, and we often feel as if we are meeting parts of ourselves for the very first time. This is what makes us feel so alive.

As I conceived of this chapter, I wanted to entitle it something that would let you know that chanting was its theme. And, indeed, as the chapter progresses I am going to lead you in writing your own chants. But when I wrote the title, I was led to the pun you see and to the connections between *chants* and *chance*. This is a perfect example of how wonderfully cracks appear in the wall of our intentions. Since knowing what to do with such chance encounters is so important to creative work, I want to explore it in a way you may find of use as you write your own chant.

One day I wanted to type the simplest of phrases: *the waters of the river.* Instead, the phrase *the worders of the river* appeared. Instantly, I was caught by the possibilities as this creative accident of fingers and mind rolled me forward into a series of questions. *What are the worders of the river?* I thought. *What language does the river speak? What syntax makes it flow so mellifluously among rocks and roots? Does the Mississippi speak in English while the Yangtze chants in Mandarin or Cantonese? Within the life of a river, are fish the hidden meaning?*

I was using the questioning technique in a playful way to make this inquiry, and I was having a ball. But this was only my imagination's way of leading me to questions of more serious intent: *Who are the worders? Who are the worders in the river I am? Who is it that flows into a poetry of joy, sorrow, and wonder? What is it for? What is it for?*

At the time, these questions were similar to others I was asking in a more pedestrian, almost psychological way. But their poetic nature—and the fact that they spontaneously repeated in my mind like the lines of a chant—awakened my intuition until personal imagery began to fly. I became excited and knew I was about to write and enter the real depths of my yearning to know.

I began to repeat each question more consciously as a chant of its own. Sometimes I did this solely within my own mind, but at times I chanted out loud. After a while, when the images and emotions the chant generated reached a certain pitch, I started to write. It was a totally spontaneous event, and, in the end, I wrote several poems based on this unasked-for opening into my deeper self. But the real gift was that I started to chant the lines of other poems as I wrote, to discover their content and to see if they would hold. This remains a practice I use to this day.

Chanting has always been part of religious ritual. The rhythm of the chant is also part of the expressive vocabulary of indigenous peoples. African and South American tribes are often known by the particular rhythms and vocalization of their chants. Each tribe has its own way of expressing the soul of the people. The children in these communities grow up with these sounds and rhythms as part of their own bodies' self-knowledge. Their patterns can be heard in the children's games and are sometimes reflected in their physical gestures as they walk or move about. It may be surprising to hear, but to a certain extent this is also true for participants in organized religions throughout the industrialized world.

In certain ceremonies of the First Nations people of the Americas, it is not uncommon for there to be the continuous beating of a drum. I was honored to attend a powwow in northern New Mexico a number of years ago where the heartbeat of the people was played on a drum made of hollowed wood, skin, and bone. The sound it made kept company with the stars all night long:

> *A drum keeps beating.*
> *A drum keeps beating.*
> *A drum keeps beating.*
> *My life and song.*
>
> *A drum keeps beating.*
> *A drum keeps beating.*
> *A drum keeps beating.*
> *My life and song.*

This chant was written during my first encounter with the drum. As you read these simple phrases several times and feel their insistent rhythms, you may notice a certain effect on your physical being. The repetitious singing of the chant, like the beating of a drum, organizes our insides in a way our bodies know from the very beginning. It is quite similar to the beating of our own hearts. But the effect does not stop there. The continuous pulse of a chant returns us to an experience many consider primal for all members of our species: the sound of our own mother's heartbeat, the first and most consistent pattern of sound we hear.

Even before we are born the rhythm of our mother's body is the rhythm of our world. The sound of her heartbeat is the musical accompaniment of our coming into being; a nine-month song woven into every cell of our developing bodies, minds, and spirits. Since it is the sound of our world at a time of such primary significance, it provides us with a reference point that means safety, comfort, the known. When we are young, the combination of having our ear held against our mother's breast as we nurse or receive the comfort her cuddling provides is often what is needed to help calm us down. The repetition of that sound draws us into a further depth within ourselves and re-places us within the circumference of a world we feel we can trust. Most people would love to be able to return to the center of this sphere as often as they can. The all-pervasive embrace of wholeness found there is part of what we mean when we speak, spiritually, of *home.*

We know that the longing to return to wholeness is a primary yearning at the root of most spiritual traditions. Because of this, the process of return is considered a sacred journey and quest. The fact that for a considerable period of our young lives we are able to experience this return to One through the rhythmic sounding of this First Sound is a matter that has always been honored by people in sacred dance and song. Given the primacy of the mother-child connection, and the workings of the natural world, is it any wonder that the intuition of early spiritual traditions so clearly identified the power of life-giving mother with the spiritual Source of Life?

Sacred ceremony often depends upon the connection between our early lives and our longing to return. The echo of the drum, the steps of the dance, and the sounding of the chant unify our being and weave a pattern that makes it possible for us to cross over the bridge of longing to the One we truly are. This occurs because the very process by which we weave toward union simultaneously *un*weaves the fabric of our rational mind. Linear-based thought and reason have many wonderful attributes, but they are rooted in a dualistic approach to life that keeps everything separate and in its place: They *this* or *that*. They *either* or *or*. *Me* or *you*. They are so inextricably rooted in *two*, they don't know how to *one*.

Chanting undoes this orientation. Whether we chant in the style found in First Nations ceremonies, or to the hollow sound of wood striking wood frequently heard in Buddhist temples, or in the style known as davening, seen in synagogues where the person chanting may also sway back and forth or side to side, it is always the same. The repetition of the chant frees us from the strictures of our usual pattern and allows the true presence, fluidity, and spaciousness of our naked mind to come alive.

Quite a few inquiries have been made into the content of what we chant. This underscores the power of the word, with which writers and mystics are rightfully concerned. By now, many people in the West have heard the word *om*, which is sometimes spelled *aum*. Without any reference to its origins, this Sanskirt syllable has entered our popular culture and may even be the name of a perfume, despite the fact that it is sacred to Buddhists, Jainists, Sikhs, and followers of the Vedic traditions alike. According to Tibetan Buddhists, for example, when this syllable is chanted with the right attention and frame of mind as part of a chain of syllables that reads *om mani padme hum,* the person chanting awakens within her- or himself the blessings and attention of Chenrezig, the embodiment of compassion. While using a different vocabulary, the same template holds true for other traditions as well. Hindu, Buddhist, Muslim, Sufi, Jewish, Christian, Earth-based, and other traditions all perform practices that depend upon their belief in the inherent spiritual qualities of specific syllables, words, and phrases.

A story I find delightful in this regard—I certainly don't tell it with any intention of disrespect—concerns Allen Ginsberg, a practitioner of Tibetan Buddhism who introduced chanting *Om* and *Ah!* to the hundreds of thousands of people who attended his poetry readings and appearances in the 1960s and after. As I heard it, this took place during a teaching of profound import offered by a master of the Tibetan Buddhist tradition. After a series of complex and quite specific instructions had been given regarding the words, hand gestures, and vocalization of a sacred chant, the participants were asked to begin chanting and to do their best to follow the instructions exactly as given. After some time, a friend of Allen's noticed that he seemed deeply involved in the practice. He leaned a bit closer to hear the famous poet's voice, but instead of hearing the sacred chant, to his astonishment he heard the bard intoning these words in his famous New Yorkese: *eenie, meanie, minie, moe.*

Other than pure fun, I'm not sure what Allen learned from his experiment, though I wouldn't put it past him to have learned quite a bit given the nature of the man's imagination. I tell this story to propose the idea that the process of realizing and writing down a chant authentic to our own spiritual needs is not as difficult as one might think. It is the opposite. The virtue of simplicity should never be ignored for the entertainment factor of complexity. If we get too fancy, there is always the possibility that Spirit itself may step in and shut the show down.

Once again, it is time to write. Please sit and breathe quietly while allowing yourself simply to think in the direction of your spiritual life and need. Your thought could be something as simple as *Where is God?* or *Now's the time.* Some people have used the phrases *I am One* or *We are One.* Others have used more traditional phrases from their spiritual traditions but personalized them in one way or another. A poem from the First Nations tradition asks

> *Is this real—*
> *Is this real—*
> *This life I am living?*

I have chanted this as a participant in various retreats over the years and it can be compelling for reasons that I believe are clear. Please note how simple it is; yet its reach is quite profound.

After considering several alternatives, please choose a simple phrase that really speaks for you and write it down. It can help you to feel the power of repetition in your body if you follow the template I offered with my own chant, which I mentioned earlier in this chapter. If, for example, you have chosen the phrase *"We are One,"* you might write it down as follows:

We are One.
We are One.
We are One.

We are One.
We are One.
We are One.

As you write your words, say them under your breath. In this way, the chanting has already begun.

You may write this one phrase of yours with the intention of chanting it as long as you find it powerful, but you may also add one more line at the end of your repetitions to further clarify your meaning or drive it home. This is what I did when I ended my chant with the phrase *"My life and song."* It expressed a realization that came to me from within the experience of chanting and also served to separate the repetitions of the chant. Many people find that going this far in the process is completely satisfying, but others like to take one more step. They alter the phrasing of this last line at will to make room for spontaneous expression and to expand the reach of the chant. Of course, you should feel free to shape this exercise (as well as all of the others in this book) to what you need.

At this point you may find yourself wondering about the authenticity of a chant you make up yourself. After all, shouldn't a chant have some real spiritual power at the root, some sacred energy officially verified by the tradition from which it comes? This reminds me of the title of an essay by Robert Creeley, "Was That a Real Poem or Did You Just Make It Up Yourself?" As Creeley tells the story, this title was an actual question asked by an audience member after an evening of listening to Creeley reading his poems. Delicious, no?

A number of years ago I was teaching a workshop in writing from mystical Jewish symbols and themes. After I introduced an interpretation of a particular symbol, one of the participants asked, "Is what you are saying part of the tradi-tion?" Immediately, I answered what I felt lay beneath her question. "Yes," I told her. "I just said it." Everyone laughed because they understood the spirit in which I replied. We should be a bit careful, I think, and not assume that a spiritual tradition is just something handed down to us from the expe-riences and wisdom of those who have come before. No mat-ter what religion or spiritual tradition we call our own, we, too, are part of the living tradition of human spirituality. It is important that we allow ourselves to assume our proper place in the continuous creation of our traditions. A path is cer-tainly where others have walked before; this cannot be denied and should be celebrated with gratitude. But a path is also where we walk, and how we walk, and what footprints we leave behind. If we do not allow our own authentic expressions full credibility, eventually we will have helped to reduce the vitality of the traditions and our own spiritual lives.

After you have written down the words of your chant, please begin to experience what it holds by starting to chant. Of course, it is best if you are alone in a quiet place where you will not be interrupted. I ask only that as you chant, you give yourself the gift of overcoming any inhibiting self-consciousness, any strictures forbidding you to vocalize, that you may feel. The same internal guard that wants to deprive us of self-knowledge often seeks to deprive us of having a voice in any form.

You may begin by whispering the words of your chant so that even if you were in a roomful of people, only you could hear. Whisper to yourself as if the words you are saying are the very words you most need. Allow yourself enough time to become used to this. Despite its benefits, however, please do not stay in this place very long. Let the sound you make touch the air. Let your voice gain in strength so that your chant may be powerful and clear. Let the rhythms of your chant cause some movement in your body until you send this true phrasing of your spirit freely into the world. Wrap yourself within your chant like it was a prayer shawl, then unwrap the shawl.

If a vision of poetic or spiritual content wants to come in, let it come. Let it come intuitively, wildly, crazily, if that's what it wants. Greet it with your chant. Let your chant take it in its arms and dance it around the room. Do your best to hold nothing back. Give yourself over to joy. Chant as you like, move as you like, see and feel whatever it is the chant holds for you. The shamanic tradition teaches that we should sing our songs until our songs sing us. Chant until you feel this coming through. Just take a chance. Give a chance. These are the same thing, really, when we give voice to what we truly are.

After you have chanted for a while, you may find that the parts of you that have come to life are asking you to write. This is wonderful and quite natural. Chanting changes us. It opens all the channels I've discussed. The physical and emotional constraints we usually feel are often the first to be set free as we hear the sound of our own voice in sacred song. Chanting also invites our sensual instincts, our passion and sexuality, to come forward in both overt and subtle ways. These are quite powerful sources of new writing and should be given full rein to lead your writing wherever they need to go. The same is true for the images, associations, memories, and visions your chanting has brought about. Let's face it, there has been a ruckus in the house. A holy riot. Please give complete permission to every part of you that wants to speak.

After you have written, take a good look at the nature of your writing. Is it different from what you usually do? Is it the same? Can you hear the voice of the chant, if ever so subtly? The beating of the drum? Don't be surprised if you do.

When we chant, a spiritual joy moves through every part of what we are. Please take the opportunity to experience this joy wherever you go. You may chant silently to the rhythm of the subway train, or you may chant out loud as you walk through the woods. I love to chant almost everywhere I go and often do. It is a direct way for me to hear what I am about at almost any moment. Sometimes, even in the shower, I find myself chanting a holy prayer. I never plan such recitations, but when I finally hear what I am saying, I give it everything I've got. Each repetition joins the water to wash me clean, and more often than not, after drying off, I find myself heading to my desk to write.

As I close this chapter, I want you to know that no matter where you chant, the joy it can bring is accompanied by your own heart's wisdom. Listen deeply to the words. They do not come to you accidentally. They are part of the imagination's plan. Feel them at your core. Each of these words is your life and song.

PARADISE NOW

((

I have tried to write Paradise

> *Do not move*
> > *Let the wind speak*
> > > *that is paradise.*
> > > —EZRA POUND, "CANTO CXX"

I have tried to write Paradise." What a thing to say, to want, to try to accomplish. It seems so immodest, at first reading, and yet there is something so pure in the depth of yearning it expresses, something so clarifying for those of us who use writing as a pathway home, that I can only feel grateful to the poet for saying it straight.

Based on the evidence of the oldest artifacts and the most contemporary art, the idea of paradise has possessed the human imagination at all times. We have drawn, danced, and created one story after another about the nature of its existence, its attributes, and what promise it holds. We have been told how we became separated from its perfection, which was ours in the beginning, and what is needed for us to reenter its gates. A teaching I've always loved from the Jewish tradition reminds us that we are born without words or the knowledge of names (one meaning of the English word *infant* is "without word"). But just prior to the moment of birth an angel reads the universe to us in the womb. It reads the earth, the stars, the wind, and the seas. It reads galaxies, and some say it even reads the hidden names of God. The entirety of existence is revealed to every unborn child. This unifies us with the Infinite and makes us complete as human beings. According to the teaching, this angel was sent because the Creator wanted each of us to know within the fibers of our unified body, mind, and spirit the true nature of all creation, and of life.

But then the story takes an unexpected turn. At the moment of birth another angel appears who pecks each newborn in that spot central to the upper lip, leaving behind an indentation and yearning of a particular kind. In that instant each of us forgets everything we have been told, every trace of knowing the previous angel has given. (How many times have you seen someone place her finger on that very spot as she tries to think or recall?) Then, with the rush of first breath, we are born howling into the empty dome of the world.

This separation from wholeness is the source of Allen Ginsberg's cry to return to the body where he was born: the body of One. It is what lies at the root of the Judeo-Christian belief in a messiah and the hope of salvation after the fall of human beings from Eden. Had paradise not been lost, no atonement and redemption would be required. To regain and embody this primordial condition is to realize our original nature. In its own way, this embodiment answers the Zen question *What was your face before your parents were born?* In a word: *paradise.*

We usually reserve this word for life in what we call the natural world. It belongs to the realm where the wind speaks, as in the quotation that opened this chapter. It is found in the thunder of a waterfall or the hollow cry of an owl as it flies through the darkened woods. We imagine it on deserted beaches and mountaintops. Our intuition reaches for something when we visit such places, and from time to time, because we are really just reaching for ourselves, we may even be able to recognize our origin in what we find.

When it comes to our daily lives, however, the wholeness the word signifies always seems at a distance. Except for spontaneous moments of selfless contemplation or activity, we long for the completion to be found in paradise, if only we can find our way *back.* Most spiritual traditions have a way of describing the span between where we are and where we long to be. In the Judeo-Christian tradition it is called *sin,* which means that we are alienated and living at a distance from the Source, from God. Buddhism acknowledges this distance and refers to it as *missing the mark.* Until we find a way to close the gap and stop missing the mark—that is, until we fully realize what we are—we live in delusion, and our suffering may be profound.

∾

I live on an island many people consider a kind of paradise. It is not five nautical miles from the invisible line the U.S. and Canadian governments have drawn through the ever-changing sea, a line those governments have declared an international boundary. Local maps of the area show this demarcation as a series of jagged red lines zigzagging across the blue parchment. It is as if they had been made by a sword.

One day as I sat beside the rocky shoreline on the southern tip of the island, I became curious about this boundary and imagined boating out to look at it for myself. Anything large enough to put on a map must be pretty impressive, I thought, and since it was such a beautiful day, I enjoyed daydreaming my way further south. But while I dreamed, I knew that in one of the lovely paradoxes life provides, things are often less clear when you are right on top of them, and this would certainly prove to be the case had I really approached the international boundary line. Once in the water it is pretty hard to tell where one nation ends and the other begins. It's a bit like trying to pin down the horizon by sailing out to the place where your sightings convinced you it had to be.

As we all know, without any regard to political designations, the sea is just the sea. The ghostlike spray of one wave arcs skyward and becomes the body of the very next wave in the miraculous process of life transforming itself from one form to another without end. None of the waves have been told to stay on their own side of the line, or if they have been told they certainly have not listened. There is an abundance of boundary crossers playfully fulfilling their destiny as sea flowers, which is to bloom and die, bloom and die, without any regard to boundary lines at all. How lovely and simple life really can be, left to its own nature and way. How freeing from arbitrary human limitation and the need to control. How grand. Can we really find this freedom within ourselves?

Late one afternoon in early October, my son and I were exploring some coves where we like to climb among the driftwood and stone. After climbing about for a while we sat on a large boulder, alternately rounded and flattened by its long relationship with the sea. Dusk would be coming soon, and the water before our eyes glowed in that autumn light as if lit up from inside. After a few minutes of silence I looked down and saw my son's innocent hand right beside me, resting on the surface of the stone. "You know, Tai," I said, looking to catch his eye, "when you touch that stone you are touching many millions of years." He neither looked at me nor at the stone his hand rested upon, but clearly he had heard. "Oh, Papa," he said, "you know I'm always touching everything." And then, in a gesture of pure joy I can still recall from my own youth, he leaped up and ran as fast as he could toward some crows that had settled in a field behind us. I watched as his jacket flew wildly behind him like some gray-and-blue wing about to lift him into the sky.

The natural arc of his flight from sea to stone to air touched me deeply. He was so much a part of the world he moved through that it left no doubt he is always touching everything. We all are. It is the everything of which all things are made. To know it is to realize the very "intimacy with all things" Zen master Dōgen wrote about in the thirteenth century when describing enlightenment. It is the jeweled net of

Indra the Hindus created to illustrate the oneness of all existence. It is the interdependent root of Jesus' declaration, *"This
bread is my body, this wine is my blood."* It is the source of life
all things share.

Every child remains in touch with this until we are
taught to memorize artificial boundaries made by the dualistic
mind. Even when we are adults, our longing proves that we do
not completely forget. No matter how doubtful or vague it
may seem, we still know what the angel read just before we
were born. We know that the entirety of life is *our* life, the life
of paradise for real.

Before he died in 1955, Père Pierre Teilhard de Chardin, or
Father Teilhard as he was sometimes known, combined his
contemplative life as a Catholic priest with his intuitive and
speculative life as a devoted naturalist-philosopher to explore
the nature of existence. His inquiry led him to possess an
absolute conviction that the unity of creation will be found by
following either path of the spiritual-scientific divide. He also
believed without question that each separate camp included
the other within its realm. Needless to say, his life path was
not made easy by the integrity he brought to his investiga-
tions. As with other mystics and intuitive scientific geniuses
before him, the profundity of his impolitic vision cost him
dearly.

However, this "catcher of souls," as he was affectionately
known, never lost his love for the natural world, which
included all beings, sentient and insentient alike. He also
never lost his love for God. Until his final days, Father Teil-

hard continued to work with a great and urgent devotion because he believed that the day was coming when *"humanity will realise that biologically it is faced with a choice between suicide and adoration"* and he yearned to help humanity make the right choice. *"My skill as a philosopher may be greater or less,"* he wrote, *"but one fact will always remain, that an average man of the twentieth century, just because he shared normally in the ideas and interests of his time, was able to attain a balanced interior life only in a scientifically integrated concept of the world and of Christ; and that therein he found peace and limitless scope for his being to expand. Today, my faith in God is sounder, and my faith in the world stronger, than ever."*

As you may imagine, he did everything he could to help others find the peace such a balance brought to his own wartorn days. When he died, on Easter Sunday, it was recalled that he had written: *"Lord, since with every instinct of my being and through all the changing fortunes of my life, it is you whom I have ever sought, you whom I have set at the heart of universal matter, it will be in a resplendence which shines through all things and in which all things are ablaze, that I shall have the felicity of closing my eyes."*

The Infinite *"at the heart of universal matter . . . a resplendence which shines through all things and in which all things are ablaze."* Is this not what we are told Moses saw on top of Mount Sinai? Is this not the spark of the Divine the teachings tell us resides in all things? And is this not also what those who are still "always touching everything" see with their unveiled hearts and eyes? I believe it is.

There is hope to be found here for each of us. This is especially true when we include a statement Father Teilhard made that I hold dear because it is such a clear and concise arrow pointing in the direction of paradise, the wholeness that we already are.

> *Traced as far as possible in the direction of their origins, the last fibres of the human aggregate are lost to view and are merged in our eyes with the very stuff of the universe.*

This is oneness. This is our nature. The truth this statement conveys has the ability to lead us in the direction home. It means that no matter where we go, and no matter what we encounter, we are always meeting our self, our Big Self. It calls to mind once again Tozan's lines:

> *When you understand self which includes everything,*
> *You have your true way.*

This applies whether we are looking at a tree that helps create the oxygen we breathe, or eating food that will become our literal flesh and bones. It is just as true for the rain that moistens our eyes as it is for galaxies of stars, the body of the Sun, the dust of space, and the blackness of the blackest holes. We are every molecule in the vastness of things that comprise universe upon universe without end. What appears to be our small life depends upon these incalculable universes working exactly as they do. Remove the sunlight from our universe, or the stars, or the wind, or the atoms of earth that constellate to make rocks and rivers and mountains and trees, and we cannot exist as we are for one moment. Even the ever-continuous present that we divide up and call time is part of who and what we are. Without it there is no one, and no thing, at all.

A useful method for making peace depends upon this foundation. It is taught by Vietnamese Zen master and peace worker Thich Nhat Hanh and has helped to bring healing into people's lives. Once each side in a conflict realizes how the interwoven fabric of existence really works, they come to see how integral the other side is to their existence. If you live in the Northern Hemisphere, Thich Nhat Hanh teaches, imagine the Southern Hemisphere disappearing and see if you will continue to exist as you are without it. If you live on the west side of the street, imagine standing at your window as the east side suddenly dissolves and see if you will still be standing on what you believed to be solid ground.

Once you participate in this exercise you will know the quite pragmatic significance of interdependence, which many scientists and mystics agree is the natural process by which all things come into existence and maintain their lives. Interdependence is genesis, they say, and thanks to nature's way—or, if you like, the Way of the Infinite—each of us can say *I am*. Once you know what *I* really includes, you may join those of us who say, "*I am* is paradise enough for me."

One day during a retreat in the mountains with Thich Nhat Hanh, he asked that each of us look at one of our hands and ask ourselves how long it had been here. I ask you to do this now. Please look at your own hand once again and ask yourself how long it has been in the world. Part of this inquiry is to ask what has brought your hand into existence and kept it alive. I am sure you will be able to easily include the entire list I offered earlier, but look for yourselves. What more do you see? Take a few moments to ask this question and jot down a few notes to use later on.

Your hand is certainly made possible by all the elements I've noted. All things are. Any time you find yourself hoping to be amazed, just remember this fact and amazement will not be far behind. But these hands of ours also hold discrete and quite specific human histories that can be traced as well. For example, it is fairly easy to trace the existence of your hand to your mother and father. You may even see in the physical details of your fingers and palm attributes you share. But if you continue to look, you will also see every ancestor in your family line. Each of these people are alive in your hand right now. Without them, and the precise lives they lived, this hand of yours would not exist. When I look at my hand, I see my grandfather who was a tinsmith and his father who was a blacksmith and my grandmother who was one of thirteen children raised on a farm. I hear the ringing of the hammer as it strikes the anvil. I see the chores each of my grandaunts and granduncles had to do as children to keep the family alive. All of this is right here in the life of my hand.

Please look at your hand and recall what you know of your human ancestors. What hardships or good fortune did they have that contributed to the life of the hand before you? What dreams or hopes of theirs do you hold in your hand today? What historical events might your great-grandmother have lived through that continue to live within you now?

What sounds of forest or city are here? What *life* is in the shape and structure of your bones, the surface of your skin? Please look carefully. To what might those lifelines in your hand really lead if you trace them to their personal origin?

Once you have looked at your hand from this perspective for a while, allow a serious and playful imagination of the real life history of your hand to freely associate throughout your heart and mind. Of course, pay attention to the literal details as you do, but make room for possibility as well. The ability for the literal truth to work together with the inexact yet compelling truth of our feelings and imagination makes for an unbeatable combination. This has been known to create some of the truest literature we know. Please begin to write a deeply imagined history of your hand. As you do, trace its details back as far as you can and then take one more step and begin to imagine what might have come just before. Give yourself some room to imagine or dream as you do this, just as I did with the international boundary. There is often more truth in imaginings than we let in, and your writing will help make this known when you surrender as you write.

After you have done this exercise, you may like to do another. The next approach asks you to consider how a new creative biography of your hand may help you to express paradise as you find it in your current life. In the thirteenth century, Dōgen wrote,

> *No creature ever falls short of its own completion;*
> *wherever it stands it does not fail to cover the ground.*

When you combine Dōgen's teaching of our original and ever-present wholeness with Teilhard de Chardin's profound sense of there being *"a resplendence which shines through all things and in which all things are ablaze,"* I think you will see why I say paradise is already here. Please consider this deeply to help generate new writing, but don't be surprised if at first you experience a bit of reluctance to really accept this. You may even feel a certain amount of fear. In part, this is because right here in your own hand you are touching something that can set you free. Nelson Mandela's famous statement that what we fear most is our own brilliance does have a strong foundation in human experience. When you write, please concentrate lightly on your hand with these quotations from Teilhard de Chardin, Dōgen, and Mandela in mind and be sure to allow for the emergence of both longing and its satisfaction. Allow for the possibility that you can find within your own wholeness the shining resplendence that Father Teilhard wrote about with such conviction and love. Imagine it is really true; and when you do, let it touch you for real. Then give as full a voice to it in your writing as you can. If your imagination reaches toward epiphany, let it do so, but do not hold this out as a goal while shying away from conflict and doubt. In writing, as in life, one often leads to the other, so we must have confidence in the process to help us write what is real. Besides, as we all know, life can be both miraculous *and* impossible.

If you do your best to allow the naked humility of *"I have tried to write Paradise"* to lead your writing, things will go well. It is a very forgiving statement. When Pound wrote *"Do not move / Let the wind speak"* he was giving us the very best of a poet's advice. Just make yourself available to whatever strong feelings, memories, or associations have come to you like movements of the wind while you read this chapter. This will help you give voice to paradise as you find it in your life.

Jakusho Kwong-roshi has written that one day when he and his four grown sons were in town together they decided to have a treat and stopped for a Coke and some fries. It was the first time in many years that they had done something like this, and to make the event even more joyous, they were accompanied by an old and dear family friend. As Roshi looked up from his food and took in those around him with his eyes, he suddenly told them that that very moment was one of the best moments of his life and that he would not want to be anywhere else in the world. This is paradise. Later on one of his sons told him that when he heard what he said, tears came to his eyes. He had never thought that a moment could be so whole.

As you can see, our experience of paradise does not have to be something complicated or grand. Often, if we just really see what we are doing, or where we are, it is enough. This is similar to Pound's instruction not to move so the wind can speak. Any scene in your own life as seemingly ordinary as the one Roshi talked about can prove quite moving and true. In one workshop where I told this story, I asked the participants if they agreed. Many of them said they did, but that it was more likely to take place in their dreams. I felt sad when I heard this and told them so. Then I said, "We don't have to rely on dreaming. If you want to experience your own whole-ness, give yourself completely to whatever you do. This stops the mental distractions that create a distance between what we really are and our lives. Just be present and real and the wind will speak. I promise. Nothing else is really required."

It is true that our mental distractions will stop when we give ourselves entirely to an activity, but sometimes it is necessary to be alone in order to stop the distractions so we can hear what the wind has to say. As a final exercise for this chapter, I'm going to suggest that you do just this: Go to a place in the natural world where you can feel comfortable and be alone. When we give ourselves this opportunity, we can encounter the world of paradise both within ourselves and in the outer world in a way that feeds our deepest yearning to know the truth of what we are.

We all have experienced times when we longed for nothing more than a period of solitude, but there are also times when we will do everything we can to prevent it. When I notice this latter tendency, I use it as sure sign that aloneness is *exactly* what I need. *"Grant me the ability to be alone,"* Rabbi Nachman of Bratzlav once prayed. *"Let my custom be to go outdoors each day so I may walk among the trees and grasses, among all the green and growing things. There, may I be alone and enter into prayer. There, may I talk with the One to whom I belong."*

One day when I went into the mountains to hear my own heart beating, as we used to say, I found myself climbing in an area I had not known before. This lack of familiarity must have triggered a sense of danger and excitement in me because I found myself extra alert to my surroundings. After a while, however, the vivid colors and shapes of the natural world awakened the vividness of my own imagination and I began to feel the unity, the intimacy, of these inner and outer landscapes. I no longer felt I walked *in* nature or *through* nature, but *as* the natural world.

As I climbed higher, I eventually found myself standing atop a large granite cliff, while above and beneath me stretched out the enormity of earth and sky. The sight took my breath away, but it also filled me with a profound sensation that I had stumbled into a sort of *rendezvous,* a moment of paradise in which my own life joined the lives of both earth and sky in a constellation I experienced as love. Before leaving, I sat and wrote the following poem.

The Tryst

On the cliff
it begins,
where land ends
meeting sky.

Grey cliff
the rock of it,
and grey sky.
All the green earth
leading there,
all one's life, alone.

When I finished the poem, I understood without question that to be "alone" on the earth is not to be isolated at all. It is to be part of the Oneness to which we belong.

Since this kind of experience provides such a profound

sense of intimacy with our world it helps to stitch paradise back into One. Many people who have known such moments have written about them in a way that has nourished their lives and mine. In order to create a similar opportunity for yourself, please take some writing materials and go to a place where you can be alone with the simple abundance of the natural world. Once you are there, sit for a few moments and allow your breathing to become calm. Let yourself feel this aloneness and, no matter what it feels like, accept it for what it is. Do not judge it at all. After some time, please stand and begin to walk. Walk slowly so that you are aware you are walking. Stay in touch with each step as you lift your foot and bring it back to the ground. Feel the movement of your body and feel the earth supporting you. This helps you to become really present where you are. When you feel solidly there, begin to look around. Look at the details of what surrounds you, including the colors and lengths of grasses, the heights and shapes of trees. Notice how the season has transformed the world in which you walk. If it is spring, notice the wild-flowers or buds. If it is autumn, notice what is still living and what has died. While you do this, let yourself also feel the breath that keeps you alive and breathe with the awareness that all of this is part of the One to whom you belong. Feel free to walk in this way for as long as you like before moving on.

In previous chapters I encouraged you to go to the natural world and practice seeing with metaphoric eyes. In this way nature became symbolic for your inner life. Then I asked you to use those metaphors in your writing. The last part of this exercise asks you to do the opposite. Please see things exactly as they occur right before your eyes and when you write them use the simple nouns or verbs that express what you see. Let trees or grass or clouds simply be themselves, just as in my experience, and the poem that came out of it, a cliff was just a cliff, the earth was just the earth, and the sky was just the sky. I did not use them as symbols or metaphors for my inner life, and I believe this "objective" orientation is why I was able to experience myself just as I was, as part of the picture: rock, sky, man.

In closing, I ask that no matter how the wind speaks in your own life, when it does, you do your best to let it speak *as you*. That is Paradise.

Then, when you write, paradise will be holding your pen. Please make a practice of working with the exercises in this chapter on many occasions. As I have noted, our psyche is always listening, always offering new ways to lead us home. Writing paradise is certainly one.

TIME TO DIE

☾

A story from the Zen tradition that has delighted me for many years concerns a rather mischievous and clever boy who lived in a Zen temple in fifteenth-century Japan. One day this young monk was entrusted with cleaning all of the ritual items on the temple altar in preparation for a special service to be held that night. According to his master's teachings, everything is the Buddha. Whether beings or objects were sentient or insentient, animate or not, the monks were to do their best to honor the Buddhas before them by giving them the care and respect deserved. Even if the monks could not yet see the Buddha in all things, they were still to consider that the Buddha was there, right before their eyes. And so, before sitting down to begin meditation, they would place their hands together and bow to their meditation cushion as a way of acknowledging the presence of the future Buddha who would be sitting there in just a moment's time. In this way they were expressing the conviction that even within themselves the Buddha was present though not yet seen.

Since he was a spirited boy who had created mischief at the temple from time to time—which caused him to be reprimanded by his teacher—the young monk was grateful to be given his first opportunity to clean the altar. He worked meticulously and remembered to approach each thing he touched as the Buddha itself. With great care he removed dust from the altar's surface, wiped the candleholders, prepared the incense burner, and placed new sprigs of flowers and some greenery in the water of the waiting vase. But despite the care and concentration he brought to his task, his hand accidentally brushed against a much-beloved teacup his master had placed on the altar for some special use. To his shock, and with a feeling of utter helplessness, he watched as the antique cup fell to the floor and shattered at his feet. To make matters worse, at that very moment he heard the distinctive step of the Zen master approaching the doors of the meditation hall.

Quickly, the boy knelt before the altar and gathered up the pieces of the cup. Then, as the large door at the other end of the hall began to slide open, he placed the broken cup behind his back and gripped it tightly in his hands.

His teacher stepped inside, bowed toward the altar, and then approached the boy to ask how things were going. In particular, he wanted to see if he had remembered to set out some special incense for the evening service. But before he could say a word the young monk asked him:

"Master, why do people have to die?"

The master looked at him with pleasure and surprise. It seemed that the boy was finally leaving behind the wasteful wanderings of his mind and beginning to wonder about the nature of reality. After all, hadn't the teacher taught again and again that the true subject of Zen is the Great Matter of Life and Death? Hoping to encourage the boy in this new direction, he answered his question in a very warm and kind manner.

"Everything has to die. Each thing has its time. Trees, grasses, flowers, all of the animals you see on the temple grounds. Someday I will die, and even you, at the right time, will meet your death."

Hearing this, the boy looked up at the master and slowly brought his hands from behind his back to where his teacher could see the pieces of his beloved but broken cup. Then he said to his teacher:

"Master, it was time for your cup to die."

And so it will be for each of us. There is a tradition whereby Zen masters, sensing their imminent deaths, will compose what will be their final poem. These brief poems often will express the understanding their lives and spiritual practices have brought them. Ikkyu, the name of the boy in the story above, lived from 1394 to 1481. It appears that as his life progressed, he must have taken the Great Matter seriously, though he was known for his unconventional behavior and approaches to Zen. Crazy-Cloud Man was the name he gave himself. In time he not only became a Zen master of far-reaching reputation, but a much-loved poet as well. Here is my version of Ikkyu's final poem, written almost eighty years after breaking his master's cup.

> *I borrowed this a month ago, just yesterday.*
> *I'm giving it back this month—today!*
> *Out of the five I borrowed I'm giving back four,*
> *So my account is clear, except for Original Emptiness.*

A number of years ago, during the time I was writing a book of poems loosely based on my meditation practice, I attended the monthlong summer practice period at Sonoma Mountain Zen Center. That summer was the hottest anyone there could remember, and on one particular day, when the temperature outside shot up to 102 degrees as we sat unmoving in our formal robes beneath the tin roof of the meditation hall, the perspiration overflowed from every cell of my body and drenched even the sleeves of my long black robe. One meditation period stifled its way into the next as I sat in the pool of sweat I had become and, to tell the truth, since my mat was in the corner of the crowded hall where not even the possibility of a breeze could find me, I wasn't sure I would survive.

At one point, hoping for relief of any sort, I mentioned this to Kwong-roshi. He smiled at me in a way I can only call incomprehensibly happy, given the heat, and said, "Let the heat be your teacher. But if you like, go ahead. Survive your life."

Finally, during a brief break from meditation in what

seemed an endless afternoon, I went outside and sought some shade. I removed my heavy robe, hoping to air it out a bit, and to ventilate myself as well. There was a plum tree not far from the rear of the meditation hall, and I hung my robe from one of the lower branches. Then I went to get a drink from the garden hose nearby. As I crouched close to the ground to have my drink, and looked back to where my exhausted robe was hanging, the following poem came to me. It isn't a death poem, in the strict sense of the tradition, but there's a quality to it I hope may be of use for the writing you will do at the end of this chapter.

> *My robe hangs in the garden,*
> *dripping like a tree.*
> *One day I'll step*
> *out of my body*
> *exactly like this.*

One afternoon in late summer, several months after my father died, my three-year-old son told me that he had seen my father more than once since his death. When I asked where he had seen him, my son told me that he usually saw him in a cloud that floated above the tall cedar as we drove down the dirt lane to our house, but that he had also seen him in a broad maple leaf that grew on a tree beside the lane. When I heard what he said, I simultaneously experienced loving my son and missing my father, and so I smiled the kind of sad smile you might imagine. I also knew that in all likelihood, my son was telling the truth. Or *a* truth, for when someone dies a new relationship begins between the ones still living and the one who has passed on. In the short time since my father's death, I had begun to feel his presence everywhere, which was not how it had been when he was alive.

Not long after this conversation with my son, I was standing beside a golden plum tree in the garden outside our home. It was filled with fruit. Conditions must have been right because as I stood beside the tree and looked at the substantial size of its trunk (our neighbor had planted the small orchard many years before), I remembered the circumstances of writing the poem about my robe. Suddenly, I began to feel myself melting again, only this time it was different. Instead of feeling the perspiration pouring out of me, I felt a kind of cool transparency suddenly overtake me from head to toe. It felt as if the substantiality of my own body was beginning to dissolve and I was slowly dematerializing like I had seen happen to the characters in *Star Trek* thirty years before. *I'm beaming up,* I thought, and laughed at this association, but I have to admit I found it interesting, even thrilling. It was fun to feel as if I was dissolving. For several minutes I stood there breathing slowly and imagining that with each breath my body grew lighter and lighter, less and less distinct as a human form, until my cells seemed to disappear into the air. My mind was very quiet as I imagined I had become part of this garden of surprise.

Then I decided to see if I could imagine myself coming back. I focused very lightly on my breath in the same slow and steady way and felt my body return to its usual feeling of solidity. When I felt completely present, I noticed I was hap-

pier and more at peace than I can say. Maybe, in some way, I
had died. Maybe I had survived my life. Maybe I had stepped
"out of my body / exactly like this," as I wrote in the poem. Each
of these possibilities occurred to me. I also knew it was likely I
was just a man standing quietly in a garden with his imagination delighting itself on a summer day. It doesn't really matter,
all in all. What does matter is that my first official act of
rebirth was to pluck a plum from the old plum tree and bite
into one of life's most delicious possibilities.

There is something of great value in the experience I've
just related. Since that day I've allowed myself to imagine that
I am dissolving and rematerializing in many circumstances: in
the woods, on trains, in airports and crowded stadiums, even
on line at the bank. I am happy to say it can be done anywhere. It does not depend upon any special external circumstances. All that is needed is a willingness to play in a sort of
serious manner, to breathe slowly and steadily as this particular imagination possesses our minds. Then we can die and
come back again anytime, which is a useful creative and spiritual tool as we face the Great Matter of Life and Death ourselves.

When my son told me about seeing my father, I knew he was
reminding me of a part of life that never dies. As it says in a
poem that holds a truth I cannot forget, but whose author I
have never been able to find since first writing it down:

> *Everything comes into existence,*
> *but look, returns to its source.*

Thus, vegetation flourishes and grows,
but returns to the soil whence it came.

Returning to the source is serenity;
it is to realize one's destiny.

I believe this poem may be Taoist in origin, though I can't be sure. A note I wrote beside the poem says: *"Though we seem to come and go, there is not one moment when we are truly away from the source. How could we be? Isn't it wonderful? Our destiny, what we think of as some point of future arrival, is really just where we have come from, and* are, all along. *This is what keeps us alive."*

I find this poem so affirming of life. It calls immediately to mind Teilhard de Chardin's assertion that we are *"the very stuff of the universe."* Isn't this exactly the truth my son saw once again with his imagination and eyes?

I want to offer two approaches to writing that will give you the opportunity to explore and express the Great Matter of your own life and death. The first will require a little preparation. If you have a flower garden, and it is a seasonable thing to do, please go into your garden and select a flower to cut and bring inside. If you do not have a garden, or if the season is not right as you read this, please go to a flower shop and select a flower to buy. In either case, stand before the flower, breathe quietly, and become aware that the flower you are choosing will be part of your expression of the Great Matter of Life and Death. Then, very gently, remembering the teaching that each thing you encounter is a Buddha—which you may rightly think of as a being in the process of awakening—take the flower in your hand and bring it into your home. The entire time you hold this flower, please do so with a gentleness and care you had hoped for as a child.

When you return to your home or apartment, please put the flower down, clear a special place on a table, fill a vase with water, and then stand at a distance from the vase with the flower in your hand. Look at the flower. Look at it with wide-open eyes as if you have never seen a flower before. Look at its color, its shape, its size. Look at the petals and see how they connect or do not connect to each other, to the center, to the stem. While you are looking, please breathe naturally and easily and feel free to touch any parts of the flower that appeal to you. Touch it with your eyes. Touch it with your cheek. Touch it in the way you learned when you practiced focusing softly. Touch it intuitively with your eyes completely closed as well as with your fingers. If you have chosen a rose, for example, be sure to touch the thorns that grow protectively along the sides. Use this touching as a way to come closer to what is right before you. Think about how at one point it was growing in the soil and now you are holding it in your hand. Let yourself feel whatever this may mean to you.

When you feel ready, please walk slowly, aware that you are walking with the flower in your hand, and bring the flower to the vase. All during this time, do not lose contact with the flower's life. Place the flower over the mouth of the vase and look at it one last time, knowing that very soon you will let it go. Be very alert to the entire range of feelings, memories, and associations you experience at this time. As you do this, remain aware of your breathing and especially of your exhalation, the dying breath. Then, with particular care, place the flower in the vase. Pay special attention to the exact moment when your fingers let go.

Now turn your back on the flower and walk slowly away to where you can sit and write. Feel free to write anything that comes to you for as long as you like. From time to time you may look up at the flower as a way of maintaining your connection, but at some point you may find your writing takes you far away.

The second exercise based on the stories and teachings in this chapter requires that you stand and breathe quietly in a place of your choosing. It may be inside your own apartment or home—some people have found it powerful to do this exercise while standing before a particular painting or photograph—but it may just as easily be in the natural world. In this case you might like to stand before a tree, as I did in my summer garden. The ocean or any body of water is also a good place to engage this process. It does not matter which place you choose. You may find it interesting to do this several times in a variety of places to discover any differences the diverse environments bring about.

No matter where you stand, become aware of what is before you. Use the same care and depth of observation you brought to the flower in the previous exercise. After you have made this contact, notice how substantial and solid the ground beneath you really feels. Allow yourself to feel rooted there and breathe steadily until you feel quite at ease.

We tell ourselves many things about what is needed in order for us to write; we list all the conditions we say must be satisfied before any writing of value can occur. But, in general, writing does not take any of these special conditions. It does not really take that much time, for example, or a courageous predisposition, or a clean kitchen. As I have said, writing takes concentration, which means it depends upon a center. When we allow ourselves to breathe deeply and slowly in the way I've suggested, the bridge it forms between our body and mind helps the center to develop right away. Then we can notice how our usual sense of time seems to disappear, and how the center itself produces the courage we need to go where we must go and say what must be said.

Once you have centered yourself, please engage in the same kind of playful imagination as I did when I stood before the golden plum tree. Without forcing it, follow the movement of your breath in and out, paying special attention to the dying breath, and imagine your body beginning to dissolve. You can do this by letting go of your usual feeling of solidity. Maintain visual contact with what is before you; stay in touch with your breathing and begin to feel yourself becoming lighter and lighter. Imagine that your cells are becoming weightless as your body seems to dematerialize and return to its source. You don't have to have a fully developed thought of what this source may be; in fact, it would be better if you don't have any ideas right now at all. Just allow this part of the exercise to be a matter of delicate sensation, an intuitive experience of the gradual dissolution of the physical form you usually refer to as "me."

Your experience will be heightened if you perceive delicately while engaging this imagination. Please notice what happens visually as you look at what is before you. Does it appear to have moved closer or farther away, or does it stay the same? What about the quality of light? Has it changed in any way? While you are observing, notice how your hearing of near and distant sounds may alter. Continue to focus on your breath and carefully sense your body's weight and size. Notice how your sensation of standing on the ground may change. Notice it all. After a while you may want to close your eyes and simply experience your inner world. Be very aware of your feelings when you do and take note of any images that appear.

When you feel ready to leave this behind, use your breathing as a bridge to return slowly and fully to your everyday body and mind. After you can feel yourself in the usual way, sit someplace where you will not be disturbed and begin to write, relying on the sensations and emotions you experienced during this process, as well as any of the associations that occur to you in the act of composition.

What Zen teachings refer to as the Great Matter is only great because we are. But what are we? It is the question that lingers in the background for most people until the end of their lives. It is the great mystery. Yet what we are continues to make itself known to us when we write. Every word has the ability to clarify this mystery, to speak one of our own hidden names. When we give ourselves completely to this activity by "dying" into our work, by letting our usual thoughts and feelings dissolve into the endless realm of spirit and imagination as we create something new, we can partake in a sacred joy that has been ours from the beginning. It is time to die. It is always time to die when we write or seek other forms of expression for our deepest self. Please approach your writing with this spirit now.

BULL'S-EYE!

(

Kobun Chino Otogawa-roshi was a Japanese Zen master who lived and taught in the United States from his arrival in 1967 until his death in 2002. He was also a master of *kyudo:* the way of the bow. One day, at the Esalen Institute in Big Sur, California, he was attending a demonstration of Zen archery by his teacher. After his teacher skillfully shot his arrow into the target, he invited Kobun to demonstrate his use of the bow. Kobun thanked his teacher in a gracious manner and took the bow in hand. As he did, a deep but gentle concentration began to show in his face.

He strung an arrow into the bow, drew the bowstring back, and with a demonstration of great attention and care began to turn his body away from the target until he faced the edge of the nearby cliff that dropped hundreds of feet to the sea. For the briefest of moments he stood completely still with the arrow angled at the sky, the fullness of his concentration expressed in the tense string of the bow, a tension shared by all who had gathered around. Then, like the sudden exhalation of a breath, he released the arrow and watched as it flew past the cliff into the ocean below. When it hit the water, Kobun shouted, *"Bull's-eye!"* And then he bowed.

The release of joy in that moment for everyone present was immense. It was as if the enormity of the target, and Kobun's instinctive ability to see it, opened all the doors and windows in the world. What a wonderful teaching! What a perfect antidote for our too-tight lives. Perhaps all of our targets are really as vast as the Pacific Ocean. Or, at the very least, perhaps we can approach our lives and writing as if they are.

So many of us live cloistered lives, separated from the natural world of who we are. Our lungs become airless rooms; we awaken out of breath as if we have just sprinted through our dreams, and then we continue running madly throughout the day without ever finding the time or the ability to breathe. It is as if we fear that one false step, or even one stray doubt, will cause us to lose the momentum of our stride and send us tumbling into a free fall from which we may not recover. Of course, most of us live so hurriedly and with such tight schedules only as a response to the demands and rhythms of our working lives. But there is great loss here, great sadness, and we need to name it if we are to help it change.

When we chase through life as if we are being chased, we diminish the power of many precious gifts. We lose the ability to stop and wonder, to look with naked eyes, to know with naked mind. The world is an ancient being that continually makes itself anew, and yet when we do not stop, when we do not open ourselves to what is being created right before our eyes, the world looks drained of life, like it has already taken place. We may not even see it at all as we tunnel through. How can we hope to connect with the source of our lives and cultivate the fruition and expression of our deepest self when we toss away the moment and live and love on the run? Even the inclination to use these abilities weakens with lack of use.

But more immediately, when we lose the moment, the instant in which *we are,* we lose the opportunity to free-fall like an arrow into the sea, to extend the reach of our understanding so that we may realize the countless possibilities of life and the imagination. Yet this is what happens when the pressures and routine demands of our working lives become so *second nature* that they put us at odds with the needs and joy of our *first nature*—to create and express our lives.

The habits of this second nature can be observed in so many ways. Frequently, when I ask people in my workshops to concentrate at the beginning of an exercise, many of them will squeeze their eyes shut and hold their breaths. Like most automatic gestures, this reveals the activity of their hearts and minds. I usually point out that concentration is not exactly dependent upon wadding ourselves up like wet paper—which causes a general, good-natured laughter of recognition in the group—but when we talk about it people say they feel the definite need to separate the outer world from the one within. They feel under such constant attack in their daily lives that there is no possibility of relaxing and touching the self without such segregation. And when I look at them, I have to admit I feel their tension and see their fear.

I'd like you to consider this final chapter as a letter to a friend. And so, my friend, I want to say that we don't have to be as closefisted and exacting with ourselves as I've described. We don't have to protect ourselves in a way that so definitively divides outer and inner worlds. The fear-driven idea that when we break stride and "miss the mark" all is lost—one of the most pernicious of received ideas in our culture—is based on a punishing view of human nature, behavior, and expression. There is no room in such a view for the delight of the beginner, the natural wonder of a child, or the necessary stumbling about that creativity requires. I once heard another writer remark in passing that writing was the willingness to fail. It is a comment that offers a lovely sense of forgiveness and ease. The willingness to fail, to miss the mark over and over again as we live and write, is a form of compassionate wisdom that keeps the necessary flow between so-called inner and outer worlds alive. It allows us to feel the continuous support of the creation, the ground upon which we stand and fall and stand again.

Kwong-roshi once told me that before you commit to the path, the path looks very narrow. But once you determine to walk it no matter what comes, you discover that the path is very wide. "So wide," he said, "even in the narrow places you can't fall off." When we allow ourselves to feel this kind of support, we discover that the real target of our lives is quite a bit more vast than we have imagined. We even discover that the center of that target is everywhere. Big or small, everything is *"Bull's-eye!"* when we fly into it with the willing largesse of heart and imagination.

From a Zen perspective, Kobun knew that he and the bow and the arrow and the ocean are originally one. They rise from a common source. Literally and metaphorically, then, he couldn't miss. When he released the arrow, he was only expressing this oneness. Or, since in our lives we must act, he was just returning one to One, and the flight of the shaft was just like a Sufi prayer. Of course, it could be said that his accomplishment was nothing special. Almost anyone could hit the ocean with an arrow shot from an overhanging cliff. But there is a difference in how things are done when we really know the unity of living. In the end, it did take Kobun's modesty, humor, and vision for that arrow to fly exactly as it did. It took a spacious concentration in which life's oneness could be known. The arc of the arrow was the arc of his understanding.

The vision that the target is large and the center can be found everywhere resides at the heart of many mystical traditions. Recently, in the scientific community, it has shown up as an essential element of *chaos theory*. One of my favorite expressions of this understanding is taught by eco-philosopher Joanna Macy, who has based a good part of her life and teachings on insights of this very kind. Joanna teaches that Nicholas of Cusa, the fifteenth-century Catholic cardinal, wrote that God is a sphere whose circumference is nowhere but whose center is everywhere.

I love this sensibility. Like Kobun's shot, it is spacious

and present at the same time. It reveals the concurrency, the intimacy, and the identity of *there* and *here,* *I* and *thou.* It reminds us of the spherical nature of reality, the "one world-ness" of the world of things. It evokes the boundlessness of spirit and the imagination while emphasizing the precise expression of this boundlessness in every mote of space. And, finally, it reaffirms for all of us the truth that in each moment, in every place, the powerful source of creation, the energy of origination, is at hand.

It has been said again and again and again: The source of life is omnipresent. It is both infinite and particular. It neither comes nor goes, and yet it can be found in all the comings and goings by which a life may be defined. It is the reason we can't fall off the path once we determine to travel it to the end, and it is the root of Kobun's act. For writers, it is the unobstructed room with neither windows nor doors that we need to end our cloistered lives; the room of permission, possibility, and paradise. When we allow ourselves to reach for the source, to discover and know the source within the world of what we are, we ally ourselves with the continuous activity of creation going on all around us. We draw the energy of life itself into our work and span the dual meaning of the word *original:* that first cause which brought about everything that followed, and that which has never existed before.

In light of this, we can't help but be original. It is what we were born for. To live original lives. To make original creations. To do original acts. No special, uptown, store-bought, extraordinary powers or attributes are needed. It is simply what we are. But we must attend to it. We must practice this living and creating at the source. We must care for what we are. It is our life's work. Then the energy of the origin will breathe life into each one of our creations; we, who live at the precise center of the world.

APPENDIX

The Beautiful Particulars

Among the beautiful particulars
with a naked mind

I walk in leaf shadow
which covers my head

beneath the sky,
the cool river guiding me

to a cool death so
I may hold in my heat

a temperature the universe
has known, expansive

in its contraction,
as I am

in my own small
way, breathing

what the whole universe has
brought me,

to keep me
alive—alive as the native

air on this most native planet
which spins at my feet tho

there is no causation,
only the constant whispering

exhalation
as the air flows thru.

I sigh. In the same
moment a common flicker

raps then chirps and raps
again, wanting in—

the beautiful particulars
coming clear as his beautiful

flicker's beak enters the soft wood.
Don't I in my own

soft wood want that?
Where I'm hot

where I'm wet in my most
feminine low-lying narrow passage

don't I want that?
What it opens into

as if ablaze
with that red drop

of day's rising
or falling motion?

Hot, red, wet, blue,
the moist tincture

earth or ocean's fire
the sudden soft cry

in the wood,
don't I want that?

And isn't it mine?

SOURCES AND
RECOMMENDATIONS

Being Peace and *The Heart of Understanding,* by Thich
   Nhat Hanh
A Book of Questions, by Edmond Jabès
The Book of Questions, by Pablo Neruda, translated by
   William O'Daly
Brush Mind, by Kazuaki Tanahashi and *Moon in a
   Dewdrop,* by Eihei Dōgen, edited by Kazuaki
   Tanahashi
The Cantos of Ezra Pound, by Ezra Pound
The Collected Poems of Robert Creeley, by Robert Creeley
Dharma Gaia, edited by Allan Hunt Badiner
Divine Milieu, by Pierre Teilhard de Chardin
Essential Sufism, edited by James Fadiman and Robert
   Frager

The Gift, by Daniel Ladinsky

Gratefulness, the Heart of Prayer, by Brother David
  Steindl-Rast

The Jew in the Lotus, by Rodger Kamenetz

Looking for the Faces of God, by Deena Metzger

No Beginning, No End: The Intimate Heart of Zen, by
  Jakusho Kwong

Odes to Common Things, by Pablo Neruda, translated by
  Ken Krabbenhoft

The Opening of the Field, by Robert Duncan

Pictures from Breughel and *Collected Poems,* by William
  Carlos Williams

Pieces of a Song, by Diane Di Prima

Ring of Bone, by Lew Welch

Selected Poems 1947–1975, by Allen Ginsberg

The Spell of the Sensuous, by David Abram

Ten New Songs, by Leonard Cohen

The Thirteen Petalled Rose, by Adin Steinsaltz

The Wishing Bone Cycle, by Howard A. Norman

World As Lover, World As Self, by Joanna Macy

Zen Mind, Beginner's Mind, by Shunryu Suzuki

ABOUT THE AUTHOR

PETER LEVITT was born in New York City in 1946. His poetry books include *Bright Root, Dark Root* and *One Hundred Butterflies.* He has also published fiction, journalism, and translations from Chinese, Japanese, and Spanish. In 1989 he received the Lannan Foundation Literary Award Fellowship in Poetry. A longtime student of Zen, he edited Thich Nhat Hanh's *The Heart of Understanding* and Jakusho Kwong's *No Beginning, No End: The Intimate Heart of Zen.* He has given readings and led workshops in writing, creativity, and spirituality at diverse venues during the last thirty years, including the C. G. Jung Institute of Los Angeles, Naropa Institute's *Jack Kerouac School of Disembodied Poetics,* Metivta: A Center for Contemplative Judaism, Zen Center of Los Angeles, and the UCLA Extension Writer's Program. He is currently on the faculty of Antioch University's MFA Creative Writing Program. He lives with his wife and son in the Gulf Islands in British Columbia.